PROPHECIES OF

Personal and Group Study Guide

DANIEL
made simple

HISTORICISM PR
FUTURISM 23
70 WEEKS
LITTLE HO
SECON
HO

SETH J. PIERCE

Pacific Press®
Publishing Association

Nampa, Idaho | Oshawa, Ontario, Canada
www.pacificpress.com

Cover design by Gerald Lee Monks
Cover design resources from SermonView.com
Inside design by Kristin Hansen-Mellish
Inside illustrations by Marcus Mashburn

The author assumes full responsibility for the accuracy of all facts and quotations as cited in this book.

Unless otherwise noted, Scripture quotations are from the Revised Standard Version of the Bible, copyright © 1946, 1952, 1971 by the Division of Christian Education of the National Council of the Churches of Christ in the U.S.A. Used by permission.

Scripture quotations marked ESV are from the Holy Bible, English Standard Version® (ESV®), copyright © 2001 by Crossway, a publishing ministry of Good News Publishers. Used by permission. All rights reserved.

Scripture quotation from *The Message.* Copyright © by Eugene H. Peterson, 1993, 1994, 1995, 1996, 2000, 2001, 2002. Used by permission of NavPress Publishing Group.

Scripture texts credited to NRSV are from the New Revised Standard Version of the Bible, copyright © 1989 by the Division of Christian Education of the National Council of the Churches of Christ in the USA. Used by permission. All rights reserved.

You can obtain additional copies of this book by calling toll-free 1-800-765-6955 or by visiting http://www.adventistbookcenter.com.

Library of Congress Cataloging-in-Publication Data

Pierce, Seth J.
  Prophecies of Daniel made simple : personal and small group study guide / Seth J. Pierce.
    pages cm
  ISBN 13: 978-0-8163-4948-7 (pbk.)
  ISBN 10: 0-8163-4948-7 (pbk.)
  1. Bible. Daniel—Criticism, interpretation, etc. 2. Seventh-day Adventists—Doctrines. I. Title.
  BS1555.52.P54 2014
  224'.506—dc23
                          2013035828

January 2014

Dedication

To my father-in-law, "Dad John," whose unwavering commitment to the Adventist message inspires me to commit my talents to preaching that message too.

Acknowledgments

Thank You, Jesus.

This project has been a wrestling match, and I am glad I can tap out and hand it over to others to wrestle with for a while. God has given me so many encouraging moments, both through the Holy Spirit and through His people.

Thank you to my wonderful girls, Angela, my love; Maddie, my princess; and Chloe, my "sweet chubbins" (don't worry, I'll change your nickname when you're older), who allow me to be antisocial while working on these projects at odd hours. Your support is incredible, and I couldn't do this without you.

Thank you to my elite and highly exclusive writer's group that meets every Wednesday at "the place that shall not be named in this book." Your insights and accountability have helped make sure this book crossed the finish line.

To all the scholars whose work I used—thanks for letting me stand on your shoulders.

Thank you, George Knight, for your teaching and encouragement and for being willing to read the manuscript. Thank you, especially, for liking the manuscript. It means a lot.

Thank you, Pacific Press®, for working with me—and forgiving my innovative grammar.

Tiger Paulsen, I appreciate your help in the marketing process. You do great work!

Thank you to my church's families all over the place—especially in beautiful, exotic locations I haven't visited yet. It's been too long, so you need to have us out to speak again.

It is also important to acknowledge the role of Pepperidge Farm cookies, warm drinks, and YouTube, which lent their support to me while I wrote. And, of course, where would I be without the random influences of Angry Birds, iPhone, iPad, iMac, Taco Bell, the Wesleyan quadrilateral, the Bermuda Triangle, Batman, the Pythagorean theorem, Facebook debates, no. 2 pencils, North Face, Post-it Notes, *Firefly, Sherlock Holmes,* and anyone who gives this book five stars on Amazon.com.

Also by Seth J. Pierce

You can also see/hear/read more of Seth's perspective on religion, God, and life in general on his Web site: www.sethjpierce.com.

Contents

Preface

This book has been a beast to write. Maybe the T-shirt below reveals why. It features an early Adventist prophetic chart, complete with beasts, timelines, historical dates, and Bible texts.

That T-shirt makes a good point. Adventists have a tremendous wealth of excellent scholarship on the subject of prophecy—but sometimes the way we communicate it can be overwhelming. Prophecy is a daunting subject for many people, and too often we overestimate how much they already know, or we bury the prophecy's big idea in innumerable, long paragraphs that drown the reader. This book is my attempt to simplify Daniel's prophecies without watering them down.

I expect some people will complain that I left things out or didn't go deep enough in certain places. To meet their needs, at the end of this book, I've recommended other books for further reading. Remember, this book is meant to be a stepping-stone to help people get into the conversations about the book of Daniel. My prayer is that those who read it will be able to see the big picture and then be drawn in to examine the smaller pieces of the prophetic puzzle.

Seth J. Pierce

Chapter 1
The Interpreter

Study Question

Can you think of ways people interpret the Bible without using the Bible?

_____

_____

_____

_____

_____

_____

_____

_____

_____

_____

_____

_____

_____

_____

_____

_____

_____

_____

_____

_____

_____

_____

_____

_____

One of the jobs I worked while attending college was covering the Prescott Hall front reception desk. It was a good job, as I'd usually get four short calls in a four-hour shift, and I could spend the rest of the time doing homework or chatting with friends who stopped by. However, one night I received a call that resulted in a crisis of international proportions. The phone rang, and I answered it: "Prescott Hall—how can I help you?"

A timid voice responded. "Jose?"

"I'm sorry," I said. "I didn't catch his last name. Is he a student here?"

"Jose?" asked the voice again.

OK, she doesn't speak English. That's easily fixed. There were only a few Joses in our dorms, and I knew most of them, so I knew I could find him by the process of elimination. Swiftly I punched the keys on the computer and located the mysterious Hispanic man known only as Jose.

"Here's your transfer, ma'am," I said while she asked again for what I presumed was her son. Then I transferred the call—only to be greeted by a busy signal.

"Uh, I'm sorry," I told the caller, "but his line is busy."

Now the timid voice transformed into something more irate. "JOSE!" the woman cried angrily.

She didn't understand what I was saying. The words I spoke bounced off her ears like bullets off Superman's chest. I had only one option left—I transferred her call to the women's dorm, muttering, "Let's see if they can get anywhere with this situation."

A few moments later, the phone rang again, and I answered dutifully. "Hello, Prescott desk. How may I—"

"JOSE!" the voice shrieked.

I was helpless. This caller wouldn't get off the line. I couldn't make the transfer, and apparently the only word in her vocabulary was "Jose," followed by what sounded like thirty or forty exclamation points. Panic ensured, and all was nearly lost—until my Spanish-speaking Hispanic friend Gil walked into the lobby.

"Gil," I cried, shoving the phone into his hand, "tell this woman what's going on! Her son's line is busy! She is screaming and probably thinks that we've done something to him or are hiding him somewhere, or worse!"

Gil grabbed the phone and in perfect Spanish translated what I had been trying to tell her. The crisis was defused, and eventually the anxious mother was reunited via telephone with Jose—who I hope has acquired call-waiting since then.

Sometimes we need an interpreter to understand the message.

The Bible's interpreter

In the book of Daniel, we see something that seems unlikely—a prophet confused by a message sent from God. The prophet says, "And I, Daniel, was overcome and lay sick for some days; then I rose and went about the king's business; but I was appalled by the vision *and did not understand it*" (Daniel 8:27; emphasis added).

Daniel was even more upset than Jose's mother was because he couldn't understand what God was telling him. It's just as easy for us to become frustrated when trying to understand what God wants to communicate to us today through His Word. Thankfully, there's a way that works.

The great Reformer Martin Luther once said, "Scripture . . . is its own light. It is a grand thing when Scripture interprets itself." This concept has been echoed throughout history by great Christian leaders. As a Seventh-day Adventist, I find this concept supported by a man named William Miller. One of his top three principles for interpreting the Bible states: "Scripture must be its own expositor [explainer], since it is a rule of itself. If I depend on a minister or teacher to explain it to me, and they should guess at its meaning, or desire to have it so on account of their creed, or thought to be wise, . . . then their guessing, desire, creed, or wisdom is my rule and not the Bible!"[1]

In seminary I took an exam in Hebrew and had to dissect each verb to make sure my translation was correct. It would have been easier if I could have used a Hebrew dictionary because it would have helped me with the translation. Using a German dictionary would have done nothing except score me a big fat F—and possibly a psychological evaluation. To understand Hebrew, I needed a Hebrew dictionary. So, if we want to understand Scripture, we need to look at Scripture.

Here's an example. Early on in the book of Revelation, when Jesus is having John write letters to seven churches, the text tells us that Jesus is the One who "walks among the seven golden lampstands" (Revelation 2:1). What does that mean? Does Jesus like lampstands? I don't see why He wouldn't—but there's a little more meaning here.

Golden lampstands were used in the Old Testament sanctuary (see Exodus 25:31). They symbolized light in darkness (the sanctuary had no windows). In describing the effect Jesus has on people, the Gospel of Matthew says, "the people who sat in darkness have seen a great light, and for those dwelling in the region and shadow of death light has dawned" (Matthew 4:16).

Jesus also likens Himself to "light" (John 8:12), and He even tells His followers, "You are the light of the world" (Matthew 5:14). In other words, God and His followers bring light to a dark world. So when we get back to Revelation 2:1, we can see that Jesus is likening His churches to lights in a dark world—meaning we are supposed to be sharing the hope and love we have instead of hiding ourselves away where people can't find us.

By looking at other places in Scripture that have phrases, images, and objects like those in the passage we're studying, we can get a clearer sense of what that passage or that prophecy is saying to us and where things are taking place.

In the case of Daniel, we are greeted with a myriad of time prophecies. Take a look at this important one in Daniel 8:13, 14: "Then I heard a holy one speaking; and another holy one said to the one that spoke, 'For how long is the vision concerning the continual burnt offering, the transgression that makes desolate, and the giving over of the sanctuary and host to be trampled under foot?' And he said to him, 'For two thousand and three hundred evenings and mornings; then the sanctuary shall be restored to its rightful state.' "

You may be tempted to think of these 2,300 days as twenty-four-hour days and come up with the time in this prophecy being somewhere around six years. Problem is, the sanctuary wasn't in its "restored" or its "rightful state," or "cleansed," as some translations have it, six years after this prophecy was given.

So now what?

As we will discuss more in the next chapter, prophecy uses lots of symbols for its descriptions, and symbols aren't to be taken literally. I mean, can you imagine reading Daniel 7:3—which pictures four horrible beasts emerging out of the sea—and thinking Daniel's prophecy means that at some point four monsters will run amok around the planet, ravaging everything in their path?

Maybe you do. But while I agree that it would be incredibly exciting to have a sort of prophetic *Jurassic Park,* I'm going to let you in on something. *Shhh*—hold this book up close to your face, and I'll whisper it to you:

They aren't literal beasts. They represent something else.

OK, back to the timeline in Daniel 8. The point is that the time periods in Daniel's prophecies aren't literal either. We need a different formula so we can understand when the events in these prophecies will occur. When we search Scripture for the answer, we find two texts that help us understand Daniel's time prophecies: "According to the number of the days in which you spied out the land, forty days, *for every day a year,* you shall bear your iniquity, forty years" (Numbers 14:34; emphasis added). And "I assign to you *a number of days, three hundred and ninety, equal to the number of the years* of their punishment" (Ezekiel 4:5; emphasis added).

Study Question

What is the "day for a year principle"?

_____
_____
_____
_____
_____
_____
_____
_____
_____
_____
_____
_____
_____
_____
_____
_____
_____
_____
_____
_____
_____
_____

Study Questions

How do you study the Bible?

_____

_____

_____

_____

_____

_____

How does the way you study it help you to find the meaning of difficult Bible texts?

_____

_____

_____

_____

_____

_____

_____

What could you do to push yourself even deeper into the Bible?

_____

_____

_____

_____

_____

_____

_____

_____

Both these passages come in the context of judgment decrees—as does Daniel 8 and the 2,300 days. These passages indicate that the 2,300 days are actually 2,300 years. When those years start and end is the subject of another chapter. For now, just remember that this way of calculating time is referred to as the "day for a year principle."

Because I am a pastor, I get a lot of weird phone calls, some of them about people's interpretation of the Bible's prophecies. People have called to tell me that the locusts in Revelation 9 are helicopters and that the mark of the beast in Revelation 13 referred to none other than President Franklin Delano Roosevelt—who died sixty years prior to that bizarre call. Other people have suggested the mark of the beast is a computer chip, and that the knowledge that Daniel 12:4 says shall increase refers to the latest gadget at the Apple store. I'm still waiting, though, for a call from a nut who goes to Yellowstone Park, and sees a bear with three ribs from an unfortunate deer in its mouth, and thinks he or she has spotted a prophetic beast wandering around (see Daniel 7:5).

At the time I'm writing this chapter, a popular piece on YouTube features a hippie videoing a double rainbow. While steadying his video camera, he marvels, weeps, and yells about the beautiful sight. After regaining his composure, he asks in hushed tones, "What does it mean?"

Biblically speaking, the rainbow is God's way of reminding us that He won't destroy the world via a flood again. In this guy's case, however, my first thought was, *I'll tell you what it means—it means, "Time to lay off the marijuana, my friend."* People tend to want to look for hidden and obscure meanings in various areas of life. That's true of prophecy too. But when we allow Scripture to interpret itself by giving us the clues we need, we avoid coming up with something crazy and making our faith (and our God) look dumb, unreasonable, and unstable.

CHAPTER 1 IN BRIEF

The study of prophecy is not a quest for some secret, mystical meaning—though this isn't to say that God doesn't know things we don't know or that He has no mystical qualities. Instead, God uses prophecy to reveal things to us. Matter of fact, in the Greek language in which the New Testament was first written, the word translated "Revelation" is *apokalupsis,* which means "disclosure" or "a revealing." In other words, prophecy is about God revealing His message to us in Scripture, not about His hiding it from us.

ENDNOTE

1. William Miller, "Rules of Interpretation," *Midnight Cry,* November 17, 1842.

Chapter 2
Genre

Study Question

What does *genre* mean?

_____

_____

_____

_____

_____

_____

_____

_____

_____

_____

_____

_____

_____

_____

_____

_____

_____

_____

What kind of stories do you like to read?

If you're going to sit down and enjoy a book, and you're not reading something just because your job demands it, what do you like?

If you enjoy stories centered on a man and a woman, and they spend the entire story flirting back and forth and misunderstanding each other until finally they kiss and get married at the end (and you don't gag once throughout the entire thing), you enjoy *romances*.

If you enjoy technology, such as spaceships, lasers, light sabers, alien life-forms, and a good measure of explosive action, you probably enjoy *science fiction*.

If you enjoy reading about dead presidents, ancient disputes, old recipes, and how people lived hundreds of years ago, your book of choice is *history*.

If you enjoy feeling tense, angsty, and nervous, and you like having sweat stain the armpits of your shirt, you probably enjoy *thrillers*.

Then again, if you like cowboys, then you enjoy *westerns,* and if you want to find out "whodunit," then you're a reader of *mysteries*.

Whether it's books or movies, these kinds of media are classified in *genres*. A genre is simply a style. Each style has its own rules; each kind of story works in a certain way. Romances usually don't feature zombies; westerns usually don't feature alien spacecraft (and when they do, the result isn't good); histories don't feature fiction; and a mystery means that, well, the story involves some kind of mystery. And too often people think Scripture is a mystery because they don't understand that it contains genres.

Biblical genres

The Bible contains many different kinds of writing, and it has genres all its own. In Psalms, you have poetry and song lyrics that use analogies that aren't to be taken literally. For example, King David, who wrote many of the psalms, says, "I am poured out like water, and all my bones are out of joint; my heart is like wax, it is

Study Question

What genres do you see in the Bible?

_____

_____

_____

_____

_____

_____

_____

_____

_____

_____

_____

_____

_____

_____

_____

_____

_____

_____

_____

_____

_____

_____

_____

melted within my breast" (Psalm 22:14).

Obviously, David doesn't mean he has been literally poured out like water, or that every joint is dislocated, or that his heart has melted—otherwise he wouldn't have survived to write Psalm 23. No, David is using descriptive language to communicate how awful he feels.

We use the same kind of figure of speech. When we say that something melted our heart, we mean that we feel warm and soft and fuzzy—not that one of the most important organs in our body has turned into a pile of steaming goo, leaving us for dead.

The same kind of thing happens in Song of Solomon—a book of the Bible in which two lovers are passing love notes back and forth. One of them says, "Your lips distil nectar, my bride; honey and milk are under your tongue" (Song of Solomon 4:11). Now, if taken literally, we could conclude that the woman whom Solomon is describing has a severe drooling problem and doesn't swallow her food. However, since this verse is in the genre of poetry, we can understand this to mean that Solomon thought this woman's lips were sweet for the kissing—which makes a whole lot more sense because pointing out a girl's drooling problem won't get you very far.

The Bible contains other genres too—*narrative,* for instance, which simply means description of historical events. Look at the following from Exodus 4:18–20: "Moses went back to Jethro his father-in-law and said to him, 'Let me go back, I pray, to my kinsmen in Egypt and see whether they are still alive.' And Jethro said to Moses, 'Go in peace.' And the LORD said to Moses in Midian, 'Go back to Egypt; for all the men who were seeking your life are dead.' So Moses took his wife and his sons and set them on an ass, and went back to the land of Egypt; and in his hand Moses took the rod of God."

This passage is simply describing what happened, and it includes some dialogue. Pretty basic and simple, right? There's nothing in the texts surrounding this passage that suggests it is anything other than the recording of a historical event—unless you believe the Bible isn't true.

The New Testament contains a genre that Jesus made popular. Called "parables," these short stories are nonhistorical illustrations told to make a point. One of the best-known parables is the story of the rich man and Lazarus (Luke 16:19–31). It reads as follows:

"There was a rich man, who was clothed in purple and fine linen and who feasted sumptuously every day. And at his gate lay a poor man named Lazarus, full of sores, who desired to be fed with what fell from the rich man's table; moreover the dogs came and licked his sores. The poor man died and was carried by the angels to Abraham's bosom. The rich man also died and was buried; and in Hades, being in torment, he lifted up his eyes, and saw Abraham far off and Lazarus in his bosom. And he called out,

'Father Abraham, have mercy upon me, and send Lazarus to dip the end of his finger in water and cool my tongue; for I am in anguish in this flame.' But Abraham said, 'Son, remember that you in your lifetime received your good things, and Lazarus in like manner evil things; but now he is comforted here, and you are in anguish. And besides all this, between us and you a great chasm has been fixed, in order that those who would pass from here to you may not be able, and none may cross from there to us.' And he said, 'Then I beg you, father, to send him to my father's house, for I have five brothers, so that he may warn them, lest they also come into this place of torment.' But Abraham said, 'They have Moses and the prophets; let them hear them.' And he said, 'No, father Abraham; but if someone goes to them from the dead, they will repent.' He said to him, 'If they do not hear Moses and the prophets, neither will they be convinced if some one should rise from the dead.' "

Whew! I know it was long but it's worth it. Consider the following details, which make it clear that this story isn't historical:

1. Most of Luke 15 consists of parables Jesus told, and Luke 16 begins with another story, this one about a "rich man."
2. If this is literal—meaning if it's about things that actually happened—then people in hell can see people in heaven and vice versa.
3. Even more revealing, if this story is literally true, people in hell can talk to people in heaven. That's awkward.
4. The Bible tells us that God forbids necromancy (communication with the dead; see Leviticus 19:31). So it makes no sense to request that someone be "sent from the dead" to do something good—to warn the rich man's wicked family to change their ways.

The main point Jesus makes in this story is that people with money need to be generous. He also teaches that there are some people who won't give their lives to God no matter who talks to them.

Prophetic genres

By now you should be starting to understand the concept of genre and to realize that since each genre has different characteristics, each must be interpreted differently. The study of how we are to interpret different writings is called *hermeneutics* [*her-men-oo-ticks*]. Now back to the genre of prophecy and the principles we use to understand it.

Prophecy has three major characteristics that I want you to note. The first key to understanding prophecy is described by one of my seminary professors in his book

Study Question

Why is it important to understand what genre you are reading?

15

Study Question

What are *type* and *anti-type*? (See Genesis 22:8 and John 1:36.)

_____

_____

_____

_____

_____

_____

_____

_____

_____

_____

_____

_____

_____

_____

_____

_____

_____

_____

_____

_____

_____

_____

Revelation of Jesus Christ. He states, "A very distinguishing feature of the book of Revelation is its peculiar and symbolic language. . . . [Revelation] should be approached with a presupposition that the scenes and actions are symbolic or figurative in nature, unless the context clearly indicates that a literal meaning is intended."[1] In other words, when we read prophecy, we come across symbols and strange language that we shouldn't take literally unless the text clearly tells us we should.

In both Daniel and Revelation, there's a fairly easy way to tell when symbols and symbolic language are headed our way. In both books there are cues that tell us when a prophet is entering a "vision" or a "dream," which is our clue that things may be about to get a little strange. Look at the following examples.

"In the third year of the reign of King Belshazzar a vision appeared to me, Daniel, after that which appeared to me at the first. And I saw in the vision; and when I saw, I was in Susa the capital, which is in the province of Elam; and I saw in the vision, and I was at the river Ulai" (Daniel 8:1, 2).

So, here Daniel is giving us the literal time and place where he was when he had a vision.

The very next verse says, "I raised my eyes and saw, and behold, a ram standing on the bank of the river" (verse 3). We have just made the jump to symbols. Daniel shifts from *when* he saw something and *where* he was when he saw it to *what* it was that he saw, and the symbols begin with a ram and go from there to horns, a goat, and the four winds of heaven.

Revelation follows a similar pattern. John says, "I, John, . . . was on the island called Patmos on account of the word of God and the testimony of Jesus. I was in the Spirit on the Lord's day, and I heard behind me a loud voice like a trumpet. . . . Then I turned to see the voice that was speaking to me" (Revelation 1:9, 10, 12). John tells us his literal location: he's on an island named Patmos, and he says he's there because of his telling others about Jesus. The big clue that things are moving toward symbolism comes in his statements that he "was in the Spirit" and that he heard a voice "like a trumpet." That's a form of symbolism called *simile*—when you liken one thing to something else. Next, John turns and "sees" in vision "seven golden lampstands" (verse 12), and then, like Daniel, John is seeing symbols.

So why all the symbols? Why not just speak normally?

Part of the answer may lie in the fact that the prophets were seeing future events and witnessing heavenly scenes that were so wonderful and beyond comprehension that they found them difficult to describe, so they used *metaphor*—which are when one thing is used to represent something else. For instance, if I said, "Susie is a real peach," you would think of something sweet—or maybe even fuzzy. And if I said, "Bob is a dinosaur," you would conclude either that he is old or that he is rather large.

Something else to consider is that within a vision, prophets may be given a glimpse into heaven, where they see supernatural beings. John sees such creatures and says, "And round the throne, on each side of the throne, are four living creatures, full of eyes" (Revelation 4:6). He then uses similes, likening one to a lion, another to an ox, one with the face of a man, and another like a flying eagle. So, are these descriptions literal or symbolic? They may be a mixture of both; we need to be flexible on some points. Perhaps they do actually have wings, but all those eyes are symbolic, representing their never-ceasing gaze.

Another characteristic we need to be aware of is one called "dual fulfillment," which means that a prophecy may have an application at the time of the prophet's vision and another application to the future. This is sometimes called "type and antitype." A *type* is something that foreshadows (points toward) a greater reality, the *antitype.* In Old Testament times, people sacrificed a lamb for their sins; but in the New Testament, Jesus is called the "Lamb of God, who takes away the sin of the world!" (John 1:29), by sacrificing Himself on the cross. The lamb and its sacrifice are types, and Jesus and His sacrifice on Calvary are the antitypes.

The last item to be aware of when studying prophecy has to do with a viewpoint or mind-set called "historical criticism."

Historical criticism

Historical criticism is a method of study that scholars use to figure out the origin of a text—where it came from. While it uses several helpful tools, the perspective of many people who use historical criticism may be flawed. Many historical critics completely deny the existence of God and that miracles can happen. They accept their beliefs *before* they study the text. In other words, before examining what the Bible says, they have already concluded that there is no God and there is nothing supernatural in the world. Consequently, they approach the Bible as if it were nothing more than a book of stories or a history book, and they deny that there can be such a thing as prophecy because that involves the miraculous ability to know the future.

Imagine you are scientist commissioned to study whether or not children like being pushed down the stairs. Yes, I know that's ludicrous but remember that the National Science Foundation spent over half a million dollars to research shrimps running on a treadmill.[2] So, let's not be too quick to judge this important study of pushing children down the stairs.

Now let's say as you begin your study you start, not by interviewing children or doctors, by writing your paper first, making bold claims that kids loving nothing more than to fall down the stairs. You even go so far as to suggest the health benefits of pushing children down as many flights of stairs as you can. You publish your paper and let the public feast their eyes upon your amazing discovery.

Not only do you lose all your credibility but Child Protective Services has their eye on you for the rest of your life.

Study Questions

What ideas do you bring to the Bible before you've seen what it says?

_____

_____

_____

_____

_____

_____

_____

Are there good presuppositions to bring to our reading of the Bible?

_____

_____

_____

_____

_____

_____

What are they?

_____

_____

_____

_____

_____

Notes

You completely ignored interviewing kids, examining medical records of people who have tumbled down stairways, getting the testimony of others who have pushed people down the stairs and faced the consequences, and even entertained the possibility that some kids—despite your perspective—may actually *hate* being thrown down the stairs. To have a respectable answer to the assigned question, you would have to include all angles and possibilities in your research of the known facts and testimonies *before* reaching your conclusion.

Now, someone might say the reverse is true for those who believe in God and the miraculous; they come to the Bible automatically believing everything to be true. That would be like someone asking you to write a paper on unicorns and you simply stating that you believe they are real despite the fact that the only place where they're found is in fictional stories. Your case wouldn't be any stronger if you duct-taped a homemade horn on a horse, took a picture of it, and used the picture as evidence. Again, your fail would be epic.

We all have *presuppositions*—things we believe before we've studied about them. We have presuppositions regarding God when we come to the Bible, but we can consciously allow for all possibilities before we examine the evidence instead of automatically discounting one possibility just because it lies outside of our personal experience. Just because you haven't seen or experienced God doesn't mean He isn't there. One evangelist put it this way: "Would you say you know—from experience and study—that you had 50 percent of all the knowledge in the universe? How about 20 percent? Ten percent? Most of us would barely feel comfortable claiming to know 1 or 2 percent of all there is to know. Is it possible, then, that God exists in the other 98 to 99 percent that you don't know and haven't experienced?"

The answer, of course, is Yes.

CHAPTER 2 IN BRIEF

The Bible contains a variety of genres, each of which has its own characteristics. Prophecy is one of these genres, and it has many unique features we need to understand in order to interpret it correctly. These characteristics include clues that tell us when the prophetic message comes in a vision or a dream and the use of symbols and of metaphors and similes in the prophecy.

People vary in the way they approach prophecy. Some discount it before they look at it, and others believe it before they study it. The challenge is to keep an open mind, to let the Bible speak for itself, and to see its words in the light of history.

People who believe that God has inspired the prophecies in the Bible can disagree about how we should interpret those prophecies. In the next chapter, we'll take a look at the various ways people interpret prophecy.

ENDNOTES

1. Ranko Stefanovic, *Revelation of Jesus Christ: Commentary on the Book of Revelation*, 2nd ed. (Berrien Springs, Mich.: Andrews University Press, 2009), 17.

2. Tiffany Gabbay, "Update: NSF Conducts $682,570 Taxpayer Funded 'Shrimp on a Treadmill' Research," *The Blaze*, December 27, 2011, accessed August 14, 2013, http://www.theblaze.com/stories/2011/12/27/update-nsf-conducts-682570-taxpayer-funded-shrimp-on-a-treadmill-research/.

Chapter 3

Past, Present, Future—and All of the Above

One of the more exasperating educational experiences I had occurred in a kung fu school about a half hour from my house. I had always wanted to try kung fu, and since I had grown up learning from a dad who is an advanced black belt in traditional Japanese karate, I felt that I must already have some skills and understanding that would help me learn the Chinese art. But while it may be true that karate drew on kung fu hundreds of years ago, I would have had an easier time reading ancient Chinese backwards and blindfolded than I did trying to make sense of what the instructors were telling me.

The problem lay in their belief that kung fu was "caught rather than taught." Whenever I felt the urge to ask a question about what we were doing, they would reply, "Talk with the hands." When you're told over and over again to talk with your hands, your hands develop an intense feeling of wanting to communicate upside someone's head!

To make matters even worse, many of the kung fu practitioners—despite the fact that they were living in middle-class houses, shopping at Wal-Mart, and wearing Nikes—acted like they were wandering Tibetan monk philosophers. When they did deign to give a verbal answer to a question I asked, they did it in riddles.

For instance, one time I asked, "Am I punching straight?" The reply I got, in a hushed breathy whisper, was, "Think of your arms as a bow [as in the weapon]. They should be as straight as the drawstring, not curved like the bow."

What on earth was he talking about? A simple Yes or No would have been fine.

I pressed the matter, telling him that his little bow analogy was simply a restating of my question; it wasn't an answer.

"Talk with your hands," he said.

"Don't tempt me," I muttered.

About that time we switched partners, and my former partner practiced with a senior student. In a few moments, I heard the senior student stop the exercise and ask my former partner, "Has anyone ever told you the bow analogy?"

I left the school shortly after that and enrolled in a karate school where the in-

Notes

structors taught in much the same way as my father had when I was growing up. The sensei had a binder that showed what we would be learning, and he answered my questions and helped me with all of my stances, katas, strikes, throws, and warm-ups. The senior students also made themselves available for extra practice sessions, and they were willing to discuss the art openly. Both karate and kung fu are martial arts, both have traditions, and both are taught in classes with one or more instructors, but they view their subjects differently.

Similarly, although you go to only one university, that university will give you many "schools" to choose from. For example, there is the school of psychology (getting inside people's head) and the school of biology (dissecting what's inside people's heads) and the school of education (putting things into people's heads). Each school emphasizes different things, though sometimes they overlap.

This is true even of the Bible's prophecies. There are four major schools of thought about how to interpret them.

Preterism

The term *preterism* has the prefix *pre,* which I guess is also in the word *prefix.* Anyway, *pre* means what comes before—so a pre-game show happens *before* the game, and a pre-made pie is one you bought already made so you didn't have to bother making a far superior, freshly made pie for your company.

Preterism is one of these schools of interpretation of prophecy. Preterists believe that all the prophecies in the Bible happened in the past—*before* the present, in other words. (See Hastily Drawn Figure 3.1.) They consider everything in Daniel and Revelation to be history. Many people are preterists because they believe that the Bible is just a book and that nothing supernatural ever really happens. So they don't believe in prophecy.

While it's true that parts of Daniel and Revelation are about things that happened when Daniel and John were alive, if these books contain no prophecies about later times, how we can apply what they say to the lives we're living now, thousands of years later?

Hastily Drawn Figure 3.1

PRETERISM

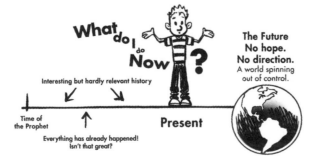

Notes

_____

_____

_____

_____

_____

_____

_____

_____

_____

_____

_____

_____

_____

_____

_____

_____

_____

_____

_____

_____

_____

_____

_____

_____

_____

_____

Futurism

Futurism is the opposite of preterism. Futurists believe that all the prophecies in Daniel and Revelation, and particularly Revelation 8–12, are meant only for the last generation of people on earth before Jesus comes (see Hastily Drawn Figure 3.2). In other words, these prophecies are all about what will happen at the end of time or just before it, and they won't make any sense to you and me until then.

Just like preterism, futurism is partially correct. It's true that Daniel and Revelation have prophecies about events beyond the time we're living in now, but that doesn't mean that none of their prophecies say anything about the past or to our time. And while we don't understand everything these prophecies contain, it doesn't make a whole lot of sense to say that we can't understand God's Word, especially what He's saying in a book titled "Revelation"—which means "to reveal" information.

Hastily Drawn Figure 3.2

FUTURISM
HEADACHE

Time of the Prophet   Present   Miscellaneous points about the far future that you can't understand, so don't even try or you'll get a headache.

Idealism

Another school of thought about Daniel and Revelation and how they should be interpreted is called *idealism*. Rather than focusing on specific points or actual events, idealists look for and cherish principles, general truths. They believe that the symbols in Daniel and Revelation say nothing about historical happenings. Instead, these books merely paint a very general picture of the ongoing struggle between good and evil (see Hastily Drawn Figure 3.3).

While it's true our application of God's Word and truth to various situations in our lives should be based on principles we find in His Word, this doesn't mean God has never given specific commands or acted in special ways during crucial times—such as when He sent His Son to die for our sins. We need to be aware of God's acting on earth during the past and the present and that He will continue to do things here on earth in the future. And we need to believe that He has given us His Word to guide us at all times.

Study Question

What are the strengths and weaknesses of each school of thought?

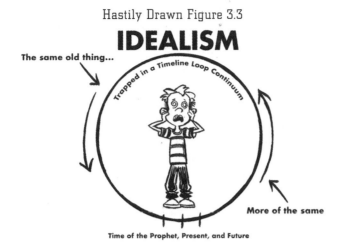

Hastily Drawn Figure 3.3

IDEALISM

The same old thing...

Trapped in a Timeline Loop Continuum

More of the same

Time of the Prophet, Present, and Future

Historicism

Finally, we arrive at the *historicism* school of prophetic interpretation. This is the school most Seventh-day Adventists subscribe to. I believe it is the best because it incorporates, in a balanced way, elements of all the schools above, and it makes the most sense.

In this school, prophecy is viewed as a continuous whole—beginning at the time of the prophet and unrolling like a scroll through history and up to the time of the end (see Hastily Drawn Figure 3.4). This means that we can believe God has been communicating during the long-ago times of the prophets, in recent history, and in the present, and that the prophecies of Daniel and Revelation give us insights regarding actual events that will happen on earth in the future. In the rest of this book, we will be looking at these prophecies from the perspective of the historicist school.

Hastily Drawn Figure 3.4

HISTORICISM

Peace from seeing that God is in control of the past, present, and future

Unrolling Revelation

God Actively Working in History

Second Coming

Present

Time of the Prophet

70-week Prophecy Fulfilled A.D. 34

2,300-day/year Prophecy Fulfilled A.D. 1844

Identity/Mark of the Beast

Time of trouble

Many people believe that the schools of preterism and futurism arose during a time when some people were interpreting prophecy in a way that portrayed the pope very negatively, and that to take the heat off him, the church of that time commissioned scholars to develop different ways of interpreting these prophecies. If all prophecy was fulfilled in Bible times, it couldn't refer to the then current pope, and that was also true if all prophecy was to be fulfilled in the future. What can we do to make sure we don't interpret Scripture in such a way as to make it say what we want it to say?

_____

_____

_____

_____

_____

_____

_____

_____

_____

_____

_____

CHAPTER 3 IN BRIEF

There probably are as many ways to approach prophecy as there are people. Individual personalities, preferences, and presuppositions can take readers in a variety of directions. However, in this book we will use the biblical concept that Daniel and Revelation contain prophecies that stretch from the times of Daniel and John and extend through the present and into the future. We can take comfort in knowing that God interacts with humanity throughout the ages and that He is at work in our lives today.

Chapter 4
Eye Exams

Study Question

Where do you see people repeating things in life to make a point?

Ever since my eyes failed me in the fourth grade, I have been subjected to the medieval medical practices of eye doctors on an annual basis. Even though my prescription hasn't changed in years, these people won't sell me anything until I pass through their gauntlet of torture.

True, I could bypass their medieval ways and go for refractory eye surgery and be done with it. However, I found out that "refractory eye surgery" is a fancy name for shooting one's eyes with a laser. Other surgeries "reshape the cornea," which is another way of saying they cut your eye with a sharp knife until you see better. I'd have better luck falling down the stairs with a sharp pair of kitchen shears. So I continue to make my sojourn to that person and his or her helpers to pester my pupils for an hour.

The first torture device of the eyeball odyssey is the eye puffer. Supposedly, this machine measures the fluid pressure in your eyes and checks for a disease called glaucoma. Whether or not you have the disease, the experience is a startling exercise in the uncomfortable. You place your head up against the machine, they tell you to look in a particular direction, and then, without warning, they blast your eye with a puff of air. *PFFFT!* The puff blows out all the moisture in your eye—along with your contact lens, if you're wearing one. By the time they puff your other eye, they have just about puffed out your patience as well.

I asked the woman who administered the test how it works, and she said she didn't know—she just pressed the button. I debated walking up to her and blowing in her eye to see how she liked it.

The next phase of this nightmare happens inside the doctor's office. Whatever pleasantries he or she greets you with are simply to set you up for the next round of suffering.

Ever since I was a kid, the people who actually cared about me told me not to look at the sun—it's so bright that looking at it can blind you, which makes sense to me. So why is it the first thing the eye appraisers do when they get you in their

What things do you view differently now than you did when you were a kid?

_____

_____

_____

_____

_____

_____

_____

_____

_____

_____

What changed your perspective?

_____

_____

_____

_____

_____

_____

_____

_____

_____

_____

office is to take a light with the power of a billion stars, hold it directly in front of your eyeball—so close that your eyelashes give it butterfly kisses—and wave this blazing source of illumination back and forth in front of your eye, sending dazzling effervescent light bouncing around in your brain?

"Yep, looks good," the light-wielding eye looker says. But the only thing I'm seeing is spots. Magical purple spots floating around the room.

Next on the docket: the Metal Facemask Lens Adjuster Machine. Used in conjunction with the MFLAM is the most tedious test ever administered to humankind. There are just two questions, which are repeated incessantly for several minutes. The first half of the question lilts upward in its inflection, and the second half descends in a monotonous—almost discouraging—inflection that makes you wonder whether you really should ever side with it.

The questions go like this: "Number o^{n}e$^?$ Or number t$_{w_{o_?}}$"

Each number refers to a different setting on the lens of the facemask that you're looking through. The eye investigator rotates through several sets of lenses as you look at a poster full of letters varying in size:

$$\text{T}$$
$$\text{H} \quad \text{I}$$
$$\text{S} \quad \text{W} \quad \text{I}$$
$$\text{L} \quad \text{L} \quad \text{H} \quad \text{U}$$
$$\text{R} \quad \text{T} \quad \text{Y} \quad \text{O} \quad \text{U} \ !$$

As you move through different lens settings, the poster changes from fuzzy to crystal clear. What a great way to mess with someone!

Well, of course, the letters don't change, but your vision becomes better and you see the letters in their entirety and in sharp focus. This process ends when the eye appraiser finds the lenses that help you see best. Then the prescription is written, you pick out your glasses or contact lenses—and you pay the bill. The final torture.

Prophetic eye exams

As we move through the book of Daniel, you'll notice that the same entities appear several times but are represented by different symbols. Studying Daniel 2's vision of the statue and then Daniel 7's vision of the various animals and finding out they mean the same thing can be confusing. The overlapping applications of prophecy can create overlapping feelings of wanting to poke your eyes out in confusion.

For example, in Daniel 2, "thighs of bronze" represent Greece (verses 32, 39). In Daniel 7, a "leopard, with four wings" represents Greece (verse 6). In Daniel 8, it's a "he-goat" with a "conspicuous horn" that—you guessed it—represents Greece (verse 5).

What gives? Is it just that Scripture is redundant?

It can feel that way—and the writers of Scripture *did* use repetition to emphasize something's importance. But in this case, the repetition is a prophetic lens check. Just as the eye doctor switches back and forth between various lenses to establish clarity, so God used differing pictures and facets of the same entity to make the reader's picture of it as clear as possible.

If I came to your house and asked to see your high school yearbook, you'd be horrified! Looking through your baby book, I'd see pictures of you from infancy to however old you are now. All the candid shots your parents took through those awkward teenage years would be on display for me to laugh at. How embarrassing for you.

I understand.

And hey, I'll do my best to laugh only at the pictures of you in the bathtub wearing bubble beards with your sister and not at anything closer to your present sources of shame.

Time changes the lens

This brings up another important aspect of the Bible that gives us ever clearer lenses to look through as we progress: things change over time.

So, there you are, reading about Babylon the "head of gold" (Daniel 2:36–38), Babylon "the tree" (Daniel 4:20, 21), and Babylon the "lion [with] eagles' wings" (Daniel 7:4, 17), when all of a sudden you notice Babylon isn't in the cast of characters in Daniel 8. As you will see, Babylon is one of the four kingdoms discussed in Daniel 2–7, but then it just drops out of sight.

The fact is, years pass between some of Daniel's visions and between some of the chapters of his book. *Years.* And at a certain point before Daniel finished writing the book, Babylon was defeated and another kingdom took its place. We'll actually see prophetic history unfold within the pages of the book of Daniel.

Remember, the historicist approach to understanding Daniel's prophecies means that we see God working in history from the time of the prophet all the way up to the very end of time. So if something seems missing, just remember that time is moving forward, and, one by one, the prophecies are being fulfilled—from Bible times to our time and into time yet to come.

CHAPTER 4 IN BRIEF

Just as we look through multiple lenses to confirm or change our eyeglass

What sort of things change your perspective on life now?

_____

_____

_____

_____

_____

_____

_____

_____

_____

_____

_____

Should Christians ever change their views of God?

_____

_____

_____

_____

_____

_____

_____

_____

_____

How do our views of God change?

_____

_____

_____

_____

_____

_____

_____

_____

What causes them to change?

_____

_____

_____

_____

_____

_____

_____

_____

Is change good or bad?

_____

_____

_____

_____

_____

_____

_____

_____

_____

prescriptions, so we look through multiple "lenses" within the pages of Daniel's prophetic book till we find the clearest picture. The changing imagery in Daniel sharpens the picture of what God is doing in history. And just as people's eyes can require lens changes over time, so, as we move through prophetic history, there will be changes in the symbols and the entities we will be studying.

While truth never changes, our understanding of it does. As we become better acquainted with God, our perception of Him and how He works will become clearer and clearer. If we aren't changing, then we aren't growing. The Christian life is never stale and static; it's constantly moving and growing. Just think how much more you know now than you did last year, and then imagine what you'll learn during the next year. I hope, in fact, that you'll learn more about Him as you read this book. May the Holy Spirit continually give you new lenses through which to see God and His plan in ever-increasing clarity!

Chapter 5
Captured
(Daniel 1)

Study Questions

Do you think it's easier to hear from God when you're comfortable or uncomfortable? Why?

_____

_____

_____

_____

_____

_____

_____

_____

_____

_____

_____

_____

_____

_____

_____

_____

_____

_____

_____

_____

_____

_____

_____

In the summer of 2007, a group of twenty-three South Korean missionaries were captured and held hostage in Afghanistan by members of the Taliban. While the missionaries probably knew the risk they were taking when they planned to travel through Ghazni Province, I wonder how many of them thought disaster would actually strike. Planning for problems is one thing, but expecting them to happen is another.

I've been in the mission field a few times and can testify to all the careful planning that has to go into such a venture. Everything from transportation to medical supplies, to food, to lodging has to be considered. Teams prepare plans of action for various crises that might arise. However, everyone goes on these trips believing that God will protect them and that despite minor setbacks, everything will work out.

However, two of the Korean missionaries were executed before a deal for their release could be reached. The remaining sixteen women and five men were kept in cellars and farmhouses for a month before they were released. Through it all, questions about their faith, about their lives, and about God permeated the makeshift prisons they were kept in. And while it would be natural to assume they praised God most after their release, Frances Chan, in his book *Forgotten God*, claims just the opposite. Here is what he discovered when he interviewed one of the missionaries: "Now that they [the missionaries] have been back . . . for a while, several team members have asked him, 'Don't you wish we were still there?' He tells me that several of them experienced a deep kind of intimacy with God in the prison cell that they haven't been able to recapture in their comfort."[1]

Setting

The closest today's children can come to being king is to head to the local Burger King, buy a kids' meal, and get a cardboard crown. While impressive in its design,

How can we know that God is still in control when the world seems out of control?

_____

_____

_____

_____

_____

_____

_____

_____

_____

_____

_____

_____

_____

_____

_____

_____

_____

_____

_____

_____

_____

the crown isn't durable and carries absolutely no authority. My daughter had a purple one, and she would—quite seriously—make several attempts to order me around. I have defied her with no adverse consequences.

In the past, some kids did better than that. Second Kings 22:1 says, "Josiah was eight years old when he began to reign." That's better than a pony ride or a pizza party at the local arcade. Surprisingly, this child king did better than his father, Amon, and his grandfather, Manasseh. Those guys led everyone away from God and created a mess, but as Josiah grew up, he made some reforms aimed at bringing his people back to God.

Then, while the temple was being repaired, the high priest found "the book of the law," Deuteronomy, which no one had seen for many years. (See 2 Kings 22:8.) They took the scroll to Josiah, and as they read it, they saw all the ways in which they were violating God's law. When they did, they ripped their clothes off.

No, seriously—that's what they did! (See verse 11.) While ripping your clothes off today could get you thrown in jail or at least could create an incredibly awkward moment, back then it was an accepted way of showing how upset you were. In any case, the nation made serious changes to be sure they were following God.

Daniel was born within a couple of years of this reformation, so he was born at a time when at least some of the people he knew had a fresh experience of serving God. Daniel 1:3, 4 says he and his friends were "of the royal family and of the nobility, youths without blemish, of good appearance and skillful in all wisdom, endowed with knowledge, understanding learning" (ESV).

In other words, if Dan were your coworker, he would be wearing designer clothes and driving a nice car; he would have been a star athlete, a chess champion, and president of Mensa. His skin would never break out ("without blemish") and all the attractive people would be drawn to him. And despite all of his advantages, he wouldn't be a snob about it. You might be tempted to hate him if he wasn't so nice to you.

But however pleasant Daniel's life might have been while he was growing up, when he was in high school, life became incredibly difficult—and not because he had raging hormones. When Josiah's son Jehoiakim took the throne at the age of twenty-five, he undid everything good that his father had done. The Bible says, "He did what was evil in the sight of the Lord" (2 Kings 23:37, ESV). The accounts of Israel's kings in books like Chronicles and Kings reveal that the vast majority of them became corrupt. Therefore, even though God had saved them from slavery in Egypt, He was going to let them be taken captive again. Daniel's hometown of Jerusalem, which had been the epicenter of the worship of God, was going to look like the epicenter of a nuclear bomb blast. God would withdraw His protection from His people and allow another power to take over.

The book of Daniel opens with an account of that hostile takeover: "In the third year of the reign of Jehoiakim king of Judah, Nebuchadnezzar king of Babylon came to Jerusalem and besieged it. And the Lord gave Jehoiakim king of Judah into his hand, with some of the vessels of the house of God; and he brought them to the land of Shinar, to the house of his god, and placed the vessels in the treasury of his god" (Daniel 1:1, 2).

Daniel and three of his friends were dragged from their comfortable lives and placed in a pagan empire that aimed to assimilate them into its culture and to strip them of every trace of faith in God. They even changed their names—*Daniel,* which means "God is my Judge," became *Belteshazzar,* "may Bel [a Babylonian god] protect the king."

The plans Babylon's King Nebuchadnezzar had for them went far beyond giving them new names. He wanted to employ them in the palace. Nebuchadnezzar and his army had destroyed Daniel's home, and now they expected him to be on their team! Nebuchadnezzar even tried to make Daniel and his friends eat what he ate.

Die-hard diet

I enjoy buffets. The thought of troughs brimming with food of every imaginable kind makes my heart rejoice. On top of that there's the fact that no matter how much you eat, the servers will continue to bring out more and more and more . . . which is why many people who frequent buffets require more than one chair to support them while they feed.

In any case, it's hard to pass up large quantities of high-quality food—especially when you've been taken captive after a siege of your hometown. When Daniel and his three friends were being briefed on their new home, the king made them a very appetizing offer. "The king assigned them a daily portion of the rich food which the king ate, and of the wine which he drank" (Daniel 1:5).

Not even Golden Corral or Old Country Buffet can compete with fare from the king's own table. No doubt the food would be the finest culinary delicacies in the land. And just think of the dessert menu! But however tantalizing the food offer was, Dan and his buddies passed on it and asked for something most people would consider a little less appetizing.

Daniel resolved that he would not defile himself with the king's food, or with the wine which he drank; therefore, he asked the chief of the eunuchs to allow him not to defile himself. . . . Then Daniel said to the steward whom the chief of the eunuchs had assigned over Daniel, Hananiah, Mishael, and Azariah, "Test your servants for ten days; let us be given vegetables to eat and water to drink. Then let our appearance and the appearance of the youths who eat the king's food be observed by you, and according to what you see deal with your servants" (verses 8, 11, 12, 13).

Vegetables? Really?

The Bible says God used Babylon to teach His people a lesson (Daniel 1:1, 2). Do you think God uses tragedy to communicate with us, or does that idea paint a bad picture of Him? Or is everything that happens to us simply the consequences of our actions?

_____

_____

_____

_____

_____

_____

_____

_____

_____

_____

_____

_____

_____

_____

_____

_____

_____

_____

Study Questions

What reasons might some-
one have for not wanting
the book of Daniel to have
been written in the sixth
century B.C.?

_____

_____

_____

_____

_____

_____

_____

_____

Why wouldn't they want
prophecy to be true?

_____

_____

_____

_____

_____

_____

_____

_____

_____

And water?

Not even water with lemon?

What on earth were they trying to do? Were they having a pity party? Had they become instant vegetarians just to be difficult?

Asking for a strict diet of water and vegetables not only raises the cringe factor for many people, but it is a massive insult to those offering you the very best of what they have. I mean, how would you feel if you invited some new immigrants to a lavish dinner, and they bypassed your gourmet spread, opting instead for a few Brussels sprouts and a glass of tap water? It appeared that Daniel and his friends were rejecting the king's generous hospitality.

What they did panicked the official in charge of their health. He pleaded with them to eat because if their health deteriorated, he would lose his head. But the Bible says, "God gave Daniel favor and compassion in the sight of the chief of the eunuchs" (verse 9). At the end of the ten days, they looked better than all the others, who had eaten the king's food.

Lots of people interpret this passage as attesting the benefits of eating a vegetarian diet and staying well hydrated, and no doubt the majority of people in North America and Europe would benefit if they drank more water and scaled back on rich foods, eating a little more simply instead. But it wasn't primarily for reasons of health that led Daniel and his crew to turn down the king's food. If they had eaten it, they would have had to violate God's instructions to His people.

For those who eat meat, the Bible points out both what meats are clean—in other words, fit to be eaten (Leviticus 11)—and how those clean meats should be prepared (Leviticus 7:26). However, Daniel and friends had no control of how the meat on the king's table was prepared, which would put them at risk of violating God's dietary laws. Second, and most important, eating food from the king's table was the equivalent of saying that the king, rather than God, was the source of life. So, by choosing a very simple diet, these faithful young men were attributing their lives and health to God rather than to the king. And the diet worked! The Bible says that "it was seen that they were better in appearance and fatter in flesh than all the youths who ate the king's rich food" (Daniel 1:15).

Most people would sink into despair at being transplanted to another land and forced to assume an identity that grates against what they value. But much like the Korean missionaries imprisoned in Afghanistan, when Daniel was a captive in Babylon, he heard God speak to him in a way he might not have had he been living in peace in his home in Jerusalem. And the words God gave Daniel in that pagan place have inspired and informed millions of people all over the world throughout history.

Date and author

According to a recently published textbook, "the traditional approach to the book of Daniel holds that a person named Daniel wrote the book in the sixth century B.C. and that it was completed toward the end of the Neo-Babylonian Empire or in the very beginning of the Medo-Persian Empire."[2]

There are many arguments for and against dating Daniel in the sixth century, and at the end of this book I have included suggestions for more reading if you are a history connoisseur and enjoy that sort of thing. However, since this is an introduction to prophecy, I won't go into those details. Suffice it to say that many people don't like dating Daniel to the sixth century B.C. because that would make the book prophetic, which doesn't fit their worldview. Some people choose not to believe in the supernatural—which includes prophecy. These people date the writing of the book of Daniel to a time after many of the predictions made in the book were fulfilled. They state that most of the predictions in the book were written after the fact, which would be kind of like taping a football game and then showing it to your friends while claiming it was a live game and then amazing them by "prophesying" the final score exactly.

However, I believe Daniel is truly a supernatural prophecy, and this book is based on the traditional dating of Daniel's book to somewhere in the mid-sixth century B.C.

Themes

The most pervasive theme in Daniel is judgment, which is essentially God's deciding right from wrong and rewarding or punishing people based on their choices. The book opens with God judging His people for their disobedience and handing them over to the Babylonian rulers Nebuchadnezzar and his successors (Daniel 4; 5). A couple of chapters later we see another judgment—God's judgment at the end of earth's history (Daniel 7:22). Of course, Daniel's Hebrew name, "God is my Judge," fits this theme perfectly.

The second major theme in the book of Daniel is God's sovereignty, which has to do with God being ultimately in control of how history and the future develop. We see this in several of the prophecies in Daniel, which reveal the rise and fall of the major empires that ruled the Middle East and much of Europe. When God judges, He is demonstrating His sovereignty—that He is in control.

Sometimes life takes unexpected and rather unpleasant turns, and you find yourself stuck in a place where you don't want to be, such as a new job, a new neighborhood, or a family that's changed because of death or divorce. It can be tempting to think God has forgotten you, but it's important to remember that you often hear God's voice more clearly in times of stress. It's the times when we feel the most hopelessly stuck and we're forced to admit that we need help that pushes us toward God, who promises to give His children what they need. He may not instantly release us from our problems; often, He gives us instead the strength to remain faithful like Daniel was when those who were holding him captive tried to change everything about him.

Daniel and his friends remained faithful to God in the midst of captivity. What challenges to remaining faithful do you face?

_____

_____

_____

_____

_____

_____

_____

_____

_____

_____

_____

_____

_____

_____

_____

_____

_____

_____

_____

CHAPTER 5 IN BRIEF

It's also important to remember that while there are consequences to your actions, being stuck doesn't automatically mean you've done something wrong and God is punishing you. It was because of the wickedness of other people and not some sin that Daniel had committed that God allowed Babylon to destroy Jerusalem and take Daniel captive. So, Daniel's life was messed up by the choices other people made. But God worked things out for him and worked through him to accomplish some incredible things. God will continue working in your life even if your life has been messed up because of the choices other people have made. May God speak to you whatever your circumstances as you study His Word.

ENDNOTES

1. Francis Chan, *Forgotten God: Reversing Our Tragic Neglect of the Holy Spirit* (Colorado Springs, Colo.: David C. Cook, 2009), 107.

2. Zdravko Stefanovic, *Daniel: Wisdom to the Wise* (Nampa, Idaho: Pacific Press® Publishing Association, 2007), 15.

Chapter 6
Cosmic Bowling
(Daniel 2)

I have come to the conclusion, after much experience, that within every set of ten bowling pins, there is one that is possessed by the devil.

Seriously.

How else can you explain how nine pins can be blown away but one is left unfazed by the impact of the ball you just hurled down a slippery lane? That pin just stands there, mocking you.

Of course, if you were lucky enough to miss it on the first throw, you have an opportunity for revenge. Many times I've found myself staring at that one evil pin that refused to be knocked down. *I need a spare. I must blow away that wicked pin that defies my authority.*

I pick up the shiny blue ball and hold it close to my chest. "Victory is ours," I whisper to it coolly. I consider the ball's silence as an affirmative and take my position in front of the lane. I stare down that rebellious pin and let a smirk twitch at the corner of my mouth. Then, with the power and grace of an Olympic shot-putter, I fling the blue orb toward my enemy, crying maniacally, "Bombs away!" as my friends look on in embarrassment.

The ball connects with the pin, the pin gives out a hollow *CRACK!* and it falls into the dark abyss into which all pins must go.

Most of the time that's what happens.

Well, at least some of the time.

Actually, most of the time the ball joins in the rebellion and heads straight for the gutter. But there's no sweeter sight than the ball blasting that infernal pin and teaching it a lesson.

Cosmic bowling

The second chapter of Daniel presents us with a dream—a vision—of a cosmic

Does God depend on us to communicate the truth about Him to other people?

_____

_____

_____

_____

_____

_____

God spoke to Nebuchadnezzar in dreams before He spoke to Daniel. Does He still speak in dreams today? What other ways might He use to prepare people to hear truth today?

_____

_____

_____

_____

_____

_____

_____

_____

_____

bowling pin and a mighty bowling ball carved from rock that smashes the pin to smithereens. Nebuchadnezzar, king of Babylon, was the dreamer.

We've all experienced nightmares, and they're scary enough. However, it's worse when we wake up with scary fragments and images, but we can't remember how they fit together—we can't remember the whole dream.

Just recently I dreamed I was in an airport with a check for twenty dollars. Sitting in the terminal was the beautiful movie star Catherine Zeta-Jones. I wanted an autograph, but there was a line, and I didn't have any paper except the check. By the time I worked up the nerve to have Catherine autograph the back of my check, she boarded her plane. I had missed my chance.

Then I woke up.

Several disturbing realities confronted me. First, I would never have anyone autograph a check. And second, I wouldn't wait till the last minute to get a star to sign something. That weird dream makes me wonder what I ate before I went to bed.

King Nebuchadnezzar had a dream too—one that he also forgot. But he considered forgetting his dream to be much worse than I usually do. Not only couldn't he remember any part of the dream at all, but in Babylon, people believed the gods communicated through dreams, and if you couldn't remember your dream, it meant you were being punished.

Since having gods angry at you is never desirable, Nebuchadnezzar called together all his dream experts, magicians, and wise men and told them, "I had a dream, and my spirit is troubled to know the dream" (Daniel 2:3).

Unfortunately, Nebuchadnezzar's people specialized in cheap tricks, scams, and fraud, so instead of using mystical powers to help him remember the dream, they replied, "O king, live for ever! Tell your servants the dream, and we will show the interpretation" (verse 4). In other words, "Tell us the dream, and we'll make up an interpretation."

The king knew what they were up to, so he gave them a few inspirational words: "The word from me is sure: if you do not make known to me the dream and its interpretation, you shall be torn limb from limb, and your houses shall be laid in ruins [the King James Version says, "made a dunghill"]. But if you show the dream and its interpretation, you shall receive from me gifts and rewards and great honor. Therefore show me the dream and its interpretation" (verses 5, 6).

How's that for a motivational speech?

Panic!

As you would expect, the king's crew panics and begin to protest, saying, "Let the king tell his servants the dream, and we will show its interpretation" (verse 7), and "There is not a man on earth who can meet the king's demand; for no great and powerful king has asked such a thing of any magician or enchanter or Chaldean.

The thing that the king asks is difficult, and none can show it to the king except the gods, whose dwelling is not with flesh" (verses 10, 11).

Note to any would-be wise men: kings don't like whiners. Whining makes them furious.

As punishment for their whininess and trickery, the king makes a decree that "all the wise men of Babylon be destroyed" (verse 12).

Imagine if someone declared that everyone with a PhD or MD was to be executed. Even if you have issues with medical doctors and universities you (hopefully) would find this to be appalling. You can imagine the frenzied panic that gripped Babylon as the guards began to round up the wise men for their elimination round in the game of life.

Daniel's decision

When things go wrong in your world, what do you do? When you discover a bill you forgot to pay—and have no way of paying it? Or when your computer plays hide-and-seek with that important file for work? What about when you get into a fight with your spouse or best friend? Are you a crier? Screamer? Do you binge eat or become violently angry?

What would you do if a city official knocked on your front door and informed you that even though you didn't do anything wrong, because of your association with a certain group of people, you now have the privilege of being hacked into pieces and having your home turned into a dung heap?

The Bible says that is exactly what happened to Daniel. Because he was trained with the Chaldeans who couldn't interpret the dream, their fate was now his as well.

Surprisingly, Daniel didn't freak out. Instead, he "went in and besought the king to appoint him a time, that he might show to the king the interpretation" (verse 16). Many people would simply be bluffing, hoping to squeeze out enough time to make it out of Babylon before the king started the killing, but Daniel was genuinely confident he—or rather, God—could provide the answers.

The next few verses show Daniel telling his friends they had better start praying like they'd never prayed before. Then the Bible says, "Then the mystery was revealed to Daniel in a vision of the night" (verse 19). A dream to interpret the dream.

The next day Daniel approached the king and declared that God had given him the answers. All the wise men sincerely hoped it was true.

If you play sports, have ever taken a test, or asked someone to go out on a date, then you know what it feels like to have anxiety. Daniel had the lives of a bunch of people hanging on whether or not he could give Nebuchadnezzar what he was looking for. This is the ultimate Final Jeopardy. So, Daniel takes a deep breath, informs everyone that God is the Revealer of mysteries, and then starts telling the king what he dreamed.

Study Question

What do you consider to be the main reason God reveals future events to humanity?

_____

_____

_____

_____

_____

_____

_____

_____

_____

_____

_____

_____

_____

_____

_____

_____

_____

_____

_____

Study Questions

A lot of people think that missionaries take God to people who otherwise wouldn't hear from Him, but the story in Daniel 2 reveals that God was already in Babylon and speaking to its ruler before Daniel said a word. What does this tell us about the role we play as witnesses for God?

_____

_____

_____

_____

_____

_____

One author suggests that we are "tour guides" who point out to people where God already is and what He's doing. What do you think of that analogy?

_____

_____

_____

_____

_____

_____

Cosmic bowling pin

Remember that demonic bowling pin that—despite your impeccable aim and the nuclear power with which you hurl your bowling ball down the lane—will not fall though the other nine pins have been blasted into oblivion? The pin that defies you? That rebellious, antagonistic, cantankerous, miserable pin that forces you to try for a spare, which you inevitably miss? The pin that makes you score a nine instead of a strike and whose subtle laughter you can almost hear over the blaring music and noise of the crowd as that evil pin is swept away to hide itself in another set of pins and ruin someone else's evening?

Yes, that pin.

Daniel says that Nebuchadnezzar dreamed of an image or statue of a man that was standing like a giant bowling pin. Rather than being made entirely of one material, this statue was divided into five parts, four being made of different metals and the fifth being made of a mixture of the fourth metal and potter's clay. At that point a huge rock, like a giant bowling ball, smashed that statue as if it were an obstinate bowling pin, turning it all into dust. And then the metaphoric bowling ball grew as big as a mountain and more, ultimately filling the entire earth (Daniel 2:31–35).

This dream is something other than a common, ordinary, run-of-the-mill nightmare. The dream is full of meaning, and Daniel informs the anxious court and king exactly what it means. In terms of genre, we move from historical narrative to symbolic prophecy with verse 36, which says, "This was the dream; now we will tell the king its interpretation."

The great statue

The head of gold. Daniel starts with the good news. He says, "You, O king, the king of kings, to whom the God of heaven has given the kingdom, the power, and the might, and the glory, and into whose hand He has given, wherever they dwell, the children of men, the beasts of the field, and the birds of the heavens, making you rule over them all—you are the head of gold" (Daniel 2:37, 38, paraphrased).

Students of history point out that gold is the perfect metal to represent Babylon. "It was the kingdom of a golden age. . . . Its metropolis towered to a height never reached by any of its predecessors."[1] Not only did Babylon have unparalleled status, but "gold was the most popular metal in Babylon. . . . The Greek historian Herodotus could not but marvel at the lavish use of gold in temples and palace construction. Walls, statues, and other objects of gold testified to Babylon's splendor and glory."[2] And elsewhere in the Bible we are told that "Babylon was a golden cup in the Lord's hand" (Jeremiah 51:7).

Babylon was definitely the head of this dream image, and no doubt King Nebuchadnezzar's head began to swell as Daniel gave the interpretation. But alas, the image wasn't just a creepy head without a body. The metals change, and Daniel tells Nebuchadnezzar his kingdom won't last forever.

The chest of silver. Moving downward, we arrive at the chest. While Daniel doesn't tell us the exact interpretation of the "inferior kingdom" that follows Babylon, he has given us the starting point, and we know enough of history to figure out who was the next world power.

We find the story of the hostile takeover in Daniel 5. This chapter tells us that Darius the Mede conquered Babylon (verse 30), which meant the gold kingdom was finished and the silver kingdom had come into power. (We'll look at Daniel 5 in greater detail in chapter 9.) The Medes were partners with the Persians. At first, the Medes were the more powerful of the two, but the Persians soon took the lead. Daniel noted their relationship when he interpreted the spooky handwriting on the wall (see Daniel 5). He told Nebuchadnezzar's grandson Belshazzar, "Your kingdom is divided and given to the Medes and Persians" (verse 28). In terms of the dream image, we can think of this part of it as the Medo-Persian pectorals.

Historians say that this kingdom of the Medes and Persians was "inferior [to Babylon] in its wealth, not in power or extent."[3] The Medes and Persians had a lot of power, and they ruled over more territory than the Babylonians did; but they weren't quite as affluent as Babylon. Again, Daniel had the details right: the "Persians used silver in their taxation system. . . . The standard monetary value for the Persians of the time was silver."[4] Here again, the symbolism in the Bible corresponds to the historical facts.

Thighs of bronze. Our next stop on our way down the line of kingdoms is at the thighs of bronze. It was Greece that replaced the Medo-Persian Empire. The Bible points out that Greece (called Javan in the text) used bronze as currency (see Ezekiel 27:13). Their military also used bronze in their armor and weapons.[5] The prophecy found in Daniel 8 says Greece was the power that followed the Medes and the Persians. We'll look at that prophecy in detail in chapter 13.

Legs of iron. In one church I pastored, we had a youth football game each fall. We had a good turnout, and many of us young adults who hold a special place in our hearts for the neighborhood games of our youth—as well as for the delusions of grandeur we have about our athletic prowess—embarked on a three-hour game that left us absolutely wasted for the rest of the week.

The worst part for many of us is that for two or three days afterwards our legs nearly ceased to function. There are precious few jobs available to adults that require hours of intense running, so our atrophied muscles let us know that they were angry by turning into jelly. However, pro football players run all day long for a living, and they can walk around the day after a game without the aid of handrails or wheelchairs. They have legs of iron.

Matter of fact, there is an athletic competition called the Ironman Triathlon that involves grotesque amounts of swimming, bicycling, and running. Conquering the Ironman Triathlon race requires incredible conditioning—legs of iron.

There is also a popular superhero in our culture known as Iron Man—based on his cybernetic suit, which enables him to accomplish great feats of strength. He, too, has legs of iron.

Study Question

How might God initiate communication with people today who don't know Him?

Study Question

Based upon Daniel's experience, how can you and I be ready to help people see what God is doing in their lives?

_____

_____

_____

_____

_____

_____

_____

_____

_____

_____

_____

_____

_____

_____

_____

_____

_____

_____

_____

_____

_____

_____

Various texts in the Bible speak of iron as a sharp implement (Proverbs 27:17) as well as something with which to destroy one's enemies: "You shall break them with a rod of iron, and dash them in pieces like a potter's vessel" (Psalm 2:9). In short, iron signifies unqualified strength and power. The kingdom following Greece, the kingdom represented by "legs of iron," would have immense strength.

While the book of Daniel doesn't explicitly name the "legs of iron" kingdom, we know enough about the previous three kingdoms to deduce what the fourth is. History tells us that it was Rome that conquered Greece and dominated the world for quite some time. In terms of culture, "the Roman army is indeed one of iron with its iron sword, shield, armor, helmet, and particularly its *pilum,* an iron spear that could also serve as a javelin."[6] The New Testament mentions Rome several times. Rome was the power that ruled the world when the New Testament was being written.

But even kingdoms of iron don't last forever.

Iron and clay. History suggests that the Roman Empire, the legs of iron, was finally worn out by a bunch of barbarian tribes. Daniel told Nebuchadnezzar what would come next: "As the toes of the feet were partly iron and partly clay, so the kingdom shall be partly strong and partly brittle. As you saw the iron mixed with miry clay, so they will mix with one another in marriage, but they will not hold together, just as iron does not mix with clay" (Daniel 2:42, 43).

I want to highlight two items for your consideration. First, notice that iron—the metal that symbolized Rome—is mixed with clay. Second, the clay is "potter's clay" (verse 41).

In Scripture, potter's clay is frequently linked with the Creator. In other words, the political situation of the world after the demise of the Roman Empire involves a unique mix of faith, or religion, and government. When the emperor Constantine converted to Christianity, he made his new faith the official religion of the state, which created the Holy Roman Empire (which didn't always act so holy toward people who disagreed with it). In other words, scholars consider the feet of the image to represent the medieval Catholic Church.

The text also speaks of intermarriages that don't work out well. This suggests that various nations would try to bind themselves with other nations through marriages, but they wouldn't be able to stick together. Think about how linked we are today in a global community in which each country's economy affects the others, and how technology has enabled us to have constant communication. Yet we still have war and disagreements and remain separate. The text also suggests that religion and government try to "marry," creating a union, but the result is negative rather than positive.

Heavenly bowling ball. Finally, we arrive at the glorious scene of the great rock becoming a divine bowling ball, which is hurled at the statue of kingdoms and demolishes them all, thus making room for one last power. Daniel says,

"In the days of those kings the God of heaven will set up a kingdom which shall never be destroyed, nor shall its sovereignty be left to another people. It shall break in pieces all these kingdoms and bring them to an end, and it shall stand for ever; just as you saw that a stone was cut from a mountain by no human hand, and that it broke in pieces the iron, the bronze, the clay, the silver, and the gold. A great God has made known to the king what shall be hereafter. The dream is certain, and its interpretation sure" (verses 44, 45).

No matter how impressive or oppressive the kingdoms of the world are, God will reign in the end, and His reign will be universal and eternal. No pin will be left standing in God's cosmic bowling alley of government authority.

With this the interpretation ends. Nebuchadnezzar praises and promotes Daniel, and he acknowledges God as the ultimate Source of power and authority.

CHAPTER 6 IN BRIEF

God can speak to anyone—even pagan kings who don't know about Him. And He can call anyone, even prisoners in a foreign country, to step forward and lead kings, queens, and presidents—and anyone else—to understand His plans. But in order for God to use us, we must seek Him, knowing that it is only by His grace that we can understand the truth and share it with others.

Nebuchadnezzar's dream revealed that history is headed somewhere. We aren't on a planet spinning out of control like some crazy broken ride at the fair. While there may be broken economies, difficult times, and cruel tyrants who hurt other people, God is letting us know that eventually He will remove all of the horrible powers that have hurt humanity, and He will replace them with an eternal kingdom that He rules and that is governed by His laws of love.

Commit yourself to seek God for understanding, because you don't know whom He is giving dreams and visions to, or when He might want you to share what you know. And don't be discouraged when times are difficult. As Daniel 2 reveals, God has a plan, and He can and will bring it to pass.

ENDNOTES

1. Uriah Smith, *Daniel and the Revelation* (Hagerstown, Md.: Review and Herald® Publishing Association, 2005), 42.
2. Jacques Doukhan, *Secrets of Daniel: Wisdom and Dreams of a Jewish Prince in Exile* (Hagerstown, Md.: Review and Herald®, 2000), 29.
3. Smith, 51.
4. Doukhan, 31.
5. Ibid.
6. Ibid., 32.

Chapter 7
A Divine Awkward Moment
(Daniel 3)

Isn't it wonderful that life so graciously provides us with multiple opportunities to experience awkward moments?

We've all had them, of course—those special times when you said something you thought was funny and no one laughed except you and then you felt a shudder of shame ripple through your body . . . which kind of tickled, so you kept laughing uncontrollably while your face turned red and your popularity points plummeted to an all-time low.

You don't plan such things—they just happen.

You talk trash about someone you think isn't around, only to discover that person is directly behind you, sobbing at your unkind words.

Awkward.

You mistake your new boss's wife for his mother.

Awkward.

You're helping lead worship at church and you're singing at the top of your lungs, when there's an interlude that you didn't know about because you missed the last practice, so while the rest of the choir observes a moment of silence, you shout out the chorus—at least until you become painfully aware that everyone is staring at you.

Awkward.

Those of us in our right minds do our very best to avoid these awkward moments. Rarely does anyone deem it necessary to deliberately take them on. We like to blend in, conform, and generally go unnoticed by society at large. We do, that is, unless we're one of those three friends of Daniel: Shadrach, Meshach, and Abednego. Those three men created an epic awkward moment that nearly got them killed.

King Nebuchadnezzar had witnessed God's power in Daniel's recovery and interpretation of his dream, but the importance of his head-of-gold kingdom impressed him more. Instead of proceeding to rule his kingdom based on the dream's revelation that it is God who sets up and tears down kingdoms, he decided to make a statement about his own superiority. "King Nebuchadnezzar made an image of gold, whose height was sixty cubits and its breadth six cubits. He set it up on the plain of Dura, in the province of Babylon" (Daniel 3:1).

Just in case you don't use cubits to measure anything, sixty cubits amounts to ninety feet. That's a big statue—and it was solid gold! At the time I'm writing this, gold fetches more than fifteen hundred bucks *an ounce*! The cost of casting a ninety-foot-tall gold statue is unimaginable.

But the cost and design aren't what's significant about this piece of art. It's what the statue stood for. It was Nebuchadnezzar's way of saying "my kingdom will last forever." In the dream, only the head was gold. The statue Nebuchadnezzar set up on the Plain of Dura was gold from head to toe. Babylon's ruler thinks he is indestructible. What's more, he wants everyone else to think that too—even if he has to kill them to convince them. "And the herald proclaimed aloud, 'You are commanded, O peoples, nations, and languages, that when you hear the sound of the horn, pipe, lyre, trigon, harp, bagpipe, and every kind of music, you are to fall down and worship the golden image that King Nebuchadnezzar has set up; and whoever does not fall down and worship shall immediately be cast into a burning fiery furnace' " (verses 4–6).

Would you expect anything less from the guy who threatened to tear people's arms off when they couldn't tell him what he dreamed?

Awkward moment

Imagine, if you will, traveling with two of your your buddies to the Super Bowl. If you've really done this, imagining it will be easy—and I'm incredibly jealous of you and trying not to despise you as I write.

Anyway, when you arrive, you discover that you and your two friends are the only people rooting for your team; the other 99,997 people in the stadium are all rabid fans of the other team. You cringe as you make your way to your seats while wearing the colors of your team. You can feel the other fans staring at you with open distaste and even hostility.

As soon as the game gets underway, the home team scores a touchdown, and in deafening approval, the crowd roars, screams, shouts, claps, whoops, hollers, and waves banners. When they finally quiet down, you and your two friends yell, *"Booooo!"*

Now, *that's* an awkward moment!

As the game progresses, your team ties the score, and it remains tied right up to the end of the last quarter. Then your team kicks a field goal as time runs out, locking in the victory, and you and your friends jump up on your seats and roar and

Study Question

What sort of images to our glory and power do we set up?

The hallmark of false religion is the use of force to make people believe things or do things. Where do you see people using force in an attempt to bring people to faith?

———————————

———————————

———————————

———————————

———————————

———————————

———————————

———————————

———————————

———————————

———————————

———————————

———————————

———————————

———————————

———————————

———————————

———————————

———————————

———————————

———————————

———————————

———————————

scream and shout and wave your banners. And then you notice that the rest of the crowd has gone menacingly silent.

A MAJOR awkward moment!

Most likely, security personnel would hurry to where you're standing and escort you and your friends out of the stadium to keep you alive. People would be flinging nacho cheese dip and drinks and hot dogs at you as you left, and the security personnel would handle you rather roughly because they also are fans of the home team. If you survived, your courage—or foolish bravado—would make the news, and you would probably be banned from ever attending the Super Bowl again.

As thousands of people gathered on the Plain of Dura, ready to bow down and worship the golden image—and indirectly, the king of Babylon, Daniel's three friends prepared to create an even more dangerous awkward moment. "Therefore, as soon as all the peoples heard the sound of the horn, pipe, lyre, trigon, harp, bagpipe, and every kind of music, all the peoples, nations, and languages fell down and worshiped the golden image which King Nebuchadnezzar had set up" (verse 7).

All except three young men.

Some of the king's men noticed. They rushed to him and said, "There are certain Jews whom you have appointed over the affairs of the province of Babylon: Shadrach, Meshach, and Abednego. These men, O king, pay no heed to you; they do not serve your gods or worship the golden image which you have set up" (verse 12).

There's nothing worse than trying to lead a worship service when no one in your congregation participates. As a pastor, I can't tell you how flustering it is when you are playing music or preaching and you can see that people's eyes are glazed over and they just stand there and don't sing. So I can understand the "furious rage" the king was feeling when he "commanded that Shadrach, Meshach, and Abednego be brought" and why he asked, "Is it true, O Shadrach, Meshach, and Abednego, that you do not serve my gods or worship the golden image which I have set up?" (verses 13, 14).

Then Nebuchadnezzar decides to be generous. He decides to give them another chance. So, before they can respond, he says, "Now if you are ready when you hear the sound of the horn, pipe, lyre, trigon, harp, bagpipe, and every kind of music, to fall down and worship the image which I have made, well and good; but if you do not worship, you shall immediately be cast into a burning fiery furnace; and who is the god that will deliver you out of my hands?" (verse 15). Nebuchadnezzar gives them a second chance to prove their loyalty in the face of death.

It's important that I interject here that this isn't fiction or a parable. It's a true story about things that really happened. In Daniel's book, Babylon was a nation—a literal political and religious power that forced people to worship in the way it specified or be destroyed. Shadrach, Meshach, and Abednego were real people who stayed true to God rather than worship images set up by humans.

One of the great themes of prophecy is worship—who is being worshiped and in what way. This story helps us to understand why in John's book Revelation, the word *Babylon* is used as a symbol of false religion. Because of Babylon's history, its name became a fitting symbol of those who oppose God and persecute His people. It's kind of like when people call your room a pigsty when it's dirty or refer to a heated argument as World War III; they're drawing on familiar, dramatic images to make their point in a strong way.

Well, back to the story and Nebuchadnezzar's government-sponsored worship initiative. The theme of the conflict about worship will become more prominent as we go on. While Daniel 3 doesn't contain a prophecy, images from the story are used in later prophecy.

They can't be serious

Nebuchadnezzar must have thought those three lunatics didn't hear the music or didn't realize the consequences of not bowing down—like when you've been calling your friend incessantly, but he doesn't pick up his cell phone because he's turned it off or put it on vibrate. The king figures the three Hebrews haven't picked up his signals because they didn't hear them correctly, so he gives them a second chance.

Problem is, they heard him the first time, and they persist in their refusal to worship. "O Nebuchadnezzar, we have no need to answer you in this matter. If this be so, our God whom we serve is able to deliver us from the burning fiery furnace; and he will deliver us out of your hand, O king. But if not, be it known to you, O king, that we will not serve your gods or worship the golden image which you have set up" (verses 16–18).

My friend Melissa Howell preached one of the best sermons I've heard based on a short phrase in the Hebrews' reply to the king. Those few words express an incredible trust in a loving God who always does the right thing.

The Message, a paraphrase of the Bible, renders the portion of the Hebrews' reply that contains the phrase this way: "But even if he doesn't, it wouldn't make a bit of difference, O king. We still wouldn't serve your gods or worship the gold statue you set up."

Did you catch it?

"Even if he doesn't . . ."

It didn't matter to those three die-hard disciples that their faithfulness might cost them their lives—their love of and trust in God was unshakable. Their faith was a stinging reminder to Nebuchadnezzar that no matter how powerful his kingdom was, he could never make everyone obey him in all things. He lacked the power to persuade these men to obey him as their god. Their faith in their God was as solid as the rock that shattered the statue in his dream.

It's hard to misinterpret comments like the one the three Hebrews made. It was quite sassy. And not only does the king dislike whining, he dislikes sass too. And

Study Questions

Does God promise to rescue us from all danger? Remember the phrase the Hebrews spoke, "even if He doesn't"? If God doesn't promise to rescue us from all trouble, why should we serve Him?

Study Question

This chapter begins our study of the major theme of the book of Daniel: false worship versus authentic worship. From what you've read so far, name at least three things that make worship false.

_____

_____

_____

_____

_____

_____

_____

_____

_____

_____

_____

_____

_____

_____

_____

_____

_____

_____

_____

_____

"force is the last resort of every false religion."[1] The Bible says, "Then Nebuchadnezzar was full of fury, and the expression of his face was changed against Shadrach, Meshach, and Abednego. He ordered the furnace heated seven times more than it was wont to be heated. And he ordered certain mighty men of his army to bind Shadrach, Meshach, and Abednego, and to cast them into the burning fiery furnace" (verses 19, 20).

Ouch.

Self-inflicted awkward moments that can ruin people's lives are inspired only by a radical commitment to something or someone that people love more than they love their own lives. This one, a big one, was motivated by their commitment to being die-hard disciples of the one true God.

The fourth Man

The car I am currently driving has no air conditioning. I hate it.

As I leave my cool office and head out to my car on a warm summer's day, I can feel the heat radiating off the dumb thing. Thanks to the all-black interior, when I open the door, stifling hot air blasts my face, and before I've even sat down in the car, I'm sweating. I drive an oven on four wheels, and I hate it.

However, when I think of Nebuchadnezzar's soldiers, I can't complain. Following the king's orders, they bind up Shadrach, Meshach, and Abednego and carry them toward the furnace, the heat pouring out from it strikes them so intensely that they barely manage to shove the three Hebrews into the flames before they collapse and die. But Nebuchadnezzar has had his revenge—or so he thinks.

But "then King Nebuchadnezzar was astonished and rose up in haste. He said to his counselors, 'Did we not cast three men bound into the fire?' They answered and said to the king, 'True, O king.' He answered, 'But I see four men loose, walking in the midst of the fire, and they are not hurt; and the appearance of the fourth is like a son of the gods' " (verses 24, 25).

Now it's Nebuchadnezzar who's having an awkward moment—he's feeling awkward in God's presence. It's like going to a party at a friend's house and running into the girl you borrowed money from and haven't repaid, or the guy you ditched while on a date, or the person you promised to help with homework but never did. That person's presence ruins the party. The presence of a fourth person in the fiery furnace deflated the king's ego and spoiled his persecution party.

The Bible adds two more miracles to the three Hebrews' walking out of the furnace unharmed. First, it says their Companion in the furnace, the fourth Man, was "like a son of the gods." Likely, it was Jesus who joined them there. And second, when the three Hebrews stepped out of the furnace, it was apparent that the flames hadn't affected them in the least: they didn't even smell like smoke. That's pretty impressive considering the way the weakest of campfires will make you stink for days.

The king was so impressed with what had happened that he praised the Hebrews' God. "Nebuchadnezzar said, 'Blessed be the God of Shadrach, Meshach, and Abednego, who has sent his angel and delivered his servants, who trusted in him, and set at nought the king's command, and yielded up their bodies rather than serve and worship any god except their own God' " (verse 28).

Not only did he praise God, but he also issued a decree. "Any people, nation, or language that speaks anything against the God of Shadrach, Meshach, and Abednego shall be torn limb from limb, and their houses laid in ruins; for there is no other god who is able to deliver in this way" (verse 29).

Because the three Hebrew men remained faithful to the one true God instead of participating in the worship of Babylon, God saved them from death and the pagan king again witnessed the power of God, who put him in his place (though, as we will see in the next chapter, the ego of the currently well-intentioned king gave him one more awkward moment—one that lasted seven years). But God is merciful, for which we can be thankful. Instead of having Nebuchadnezzar's four limbs torn from his body, He merely had him walk on all fours for a while.

CHAPTER 7 IN BRIEF

Worship is a predominant theme throughout Daniel and Revelation (and the entire Bible, for that matter). They reveal the forces of good and evil battling for people's hearts, which Daniel 3 illustrates so beautifully. Human kingdoms are in constant competition with God's kingdom.

We will always be tempted to follow the crowd and worship what culture says is God, whether it's a person, beauty, sex, money, or fashion—or even good grades and how much better you know the Bible than your friends do. As time winds down on planet Earth, we will arrive at a scene not unlike the one we just read about—one in which powerful political forces try to make people worship their way. The decision to reject their commands and continue to follow God will be a hard one—and perhaps a dangerous one as well. But in the end, it will be worth whatever happens.

Every believer should have the goal of having a faith in God that's strong enough to say, "I will obey Him 'even if He doesn't' give me what I want or protect me from all the disagreeable things that can happen to me." That kind of faith is based on *who* God is instead of on *what* God does. It's a trust based on His goodness, faithfulness, trustworthiness, and His love. Obtaining that kind of faith won't be easy. Ultimately, it must come from God.

ENDNOTE

1. Ellen G. White, *Signs of the Times*®, May 6, 1897.

Study Question

This chapter gives us a glimpse of Jesus before He took on human flesh. Where else in the Old Testament do you see Jesus?

Chapter 8
Losing Your Mind
(Daniel 4)

Many years ago the actor Jim Carrey played the role of a man who'd been called from the audience onto the stage to be humiliated by a hypnotist. A few mystical movements by the hypnotist, and suddenly Carrey takes on the mind and mannerisms of a chicken. He clucks and scratches, and the audience claps.

Then the hypnotist suffers a massive heart attack and dies before restoring Carrey to normality. Frantic, the man with the mind of a chicken clucks and pecks at the lifeless body, trying to revive him.

No luck.

Years go by, and then we see Carrey enter a burger joint dressed like a homeless person. As he approaches the woman working the counter, he's thinking, *OK, just concentrate and put the money on the counter.* But when he opens his mouth and begins to order, the only sound that escapes his lips is *"Ba-GAWK!"* The cashier is alarmed.

In a panic, Carrey grabs a piece of paper and a pen, thinking he'll be able to write down his order and quiet his starving stomach. However, when he stops writing and holds up the paper, it reads, *"Cluck! Cluck! Cluck!"* and the cashier says, "I can't read that chicken scratch!"

Animal mind

That ridiculous story parallels a real story involving King Nebuchadnezzar that's recounted in Daniel 4. In fact, the king actually wrote the fourth chapter of Daniel. In it he tells about another dream he had, this one involving a big ol' tree that gets chopped down. His dream goes like this:

"I [Nebuchadnezzar] saw in the visions of my head as I lay in bed, and behold, a watcher, a holy one, came down from heaven. He cried aloud and said thus, 'Hew down the tree and cut off its branches, strip off its leaves and scatter its fruit; let the beasts flee from under it and the birds from its branches. But leave the stump of its roots in the earth, bound with a band of iron and bronze, amid the tender grass of the field. Let him be wet with the dew of heaven; let his lot be with the beasts in the grass of the earth; let his mind be changed from a man's, and let a beast's mind be given to him; and let seven times pass over him. The sentence is by the decree of the watchers, the decision by the word of the holy ones, to the end that the living may know that the Most High rules the kingdom of men, and gives it to whom he will and sets over it the lowliest of men' " (Daniel 4:13–18).

Just as in Daniel 2, none of the king's smart people have a clue as to what the dream means, so someone calls Daniel on the scene to break it down. He says the tree represents King Nebuchadnezzar (Daniel 4:20–22). Because he has become full of himself, he will be "driven from among men" and will dwell "with the beasts of the field." What's more, the king will "eat grass like an ox" and will be "wet with the dew of heaven" (verse 25).

But good news! Nebuchadnezzar's condition isn't permanent. It's limited to "seven times," or, as some translations say, "seven periods of times" (verse 25). When the grass eating business is over, Nebuchadnezzar will be restored.

Daniel appropriately counsels, "Break off your sins," in the hope that Nebuchadnezzar can avoid this consequence (verse 27).

What kind of sins can this king who actually listens to Daniel commit?

The biblical story says that a short time later, the king was enjoying a constitutional on his rooftop and looking over his impressive kingdom. Feeling satisfied with himself, he says, "Is not this great Babylon, which I have built by my mighty power as a royal residence and for the glory of my majesty?" (verse 30). Even after hearing that it is God who sets up kingdoms and after the fiery furnace debacle, the king claims credit for what God has done.

What happens next is akin to what happens when you say something stupid, realize what you're doing as you say it, but can't stop the words. For example, if a woman asks you if an outfit makes her look fat and you respond brainlessly, "The dress isn't the problem," you're in a world of trouble. Conversely, if you're a girl who's watching a guy play football, and he makes a play and then proudly asks, "What did you think of that?" and you suggest that he "runs like a little girl" and that he's lucky he didn't "damage his willowy frame," you won't score any points with him. As you say those words, you'll realize that you've made a grievous mistake.

Nebuchadnezzar did. The Bible says, "While the words were still in the king's mouth, there fell a voice from heaven, 'O King Nebuchadnezzar, to you it is spoken: The kingdom has departed from you' " (verse 31).

Study Questions

Psychiatrists have names for the mental illness of thinking you are an ox (*boanthropy*) or a wolf (*lycanthropy*). King Nebuchadnezzar lost his mind in a dramatic way when he lost sight of God. Do people today lose their minds when they take their focus off of God and place it on themselves? In what ways?

_____

_____

_____

_____

_____

_____

_____

_____

_____

_____

_____

_____

_____

_____

_____

_____

Study Questions

Is it ever too late to find salvation?

_____

_____

_____

_____

_____

_____

_____

In what area of your life are you tempted to give yourself the credit that belongs to God?

_____

_____

_____

_____

_____

_____

_____

_____

_____

_____

_____

_____

What happens next is literally a dream come true—albeit not a good dream. The king's human mind morphs into that of an ox. Dropping to all fours, he scrambles out of the city and into the wilderness, eating grass and letting his hair grow "as long as eagles' feathers" and his fingernails like "birds' claws."

What a charmer.

How long?

Nebuchadnezzar's humiliation was to last "seven times" or "seven periods of time," which scholars understand to mean seven years. They conclude this for two reasons: First, because the Septuagint, the old Greek translation of the Hebrew scripture, reads "seven years." And second, because this chapter of Daniel was written in Aramaic, and the word translated "time" is _iddan,_ which both ancient and modern interpreters say means "year."

That this word means _year_ will become important later on. For now, just imagine an incredibly awkward moment that lasts for more than half a decade—one that will be written about and studied for hundreds of years, all because you couldn't control your big mouth and big ego. Mercifully, Nebuchadnezzar wasn't in his right mind during those years and probably didn't have much going through his head except an incredible urge to eat grass.

Nebuchadnezzar writes that when the seven years had finally passed, "At the end of the days I, Nebuchadnezzar, lifted my eyes to heaven, and my reason returned to me, and I blessed the Most High, and praised and honored him who lives for ever" (verse 34). He then goes on to write a song with lyrics that say God's "kingdom endures from generation to generation" and "none can stay his hand." The king finally has his mind restored to him, and he ends the chapter by giving praise to the "King of heaven."

Sometimes we need to lose things so we can learn to appreciate what's really important. Nebuchadnezzar was stripped of every kingly characteristic he had, but that helped him put things in perspective when his rationality was restored.

CHAPTER 8 IN BRIEF

There's a proverb in the Bible that says, "Pride goes before destruction, and a haughty spirit before a fall" (Proverbs 16:18). The idea is that when we become full of ourselves, our view of reality becomes skewed and we stumble. It may be that we brag too much about our abilities and then can't produce—or simply that we irritate everyone around us with our arrogant attitude. Whatever the case, the story in Daniel 4 reminds us that God is King and we're not—even if we have a really good life, all kinds of money we can spend on cool stuff, and a lot of talent. Careless actions or rash words can cause us to lose it all.

Maybe you've made mistakes because you've had too lofty a view of yourself and your abilities or popularity. That's OK; we've all done that—and that fact brings us to the redeeming part of this story: God doesn't leave us to wallow in our failures. Instead, He uses them to restore us. Nebuchadnezzar went crazy for seven years and looked like an idiot, but God didn't leave him there. Even though the king ignored the lessons of his dream of the statue and his experience with the golden image and the furnace, God still wanted to work in his life. When God disciplines us, it's always to redeem and restore us, not merely to make our life miserable.

Study Question

In Daniel 4:31, the phrase "has departed from you" is written in what is called the *prophetic perfect*. This grammatical term means that, while Nebuchadnezzar hadn't lost his mind yet, the event was so certain that it was thought of as already having been accomplished. What other events spoken of in the Bible can we consider to be this certain? (Read John 19:30; 1 Thessalonians 4:13-18.)

_____

_____

_____

_____

_____

_____

_____

_____

_____

_____

_____

_____

_____

Study Question

Belshazzar knew his grandfather's story, but he missed—or ignored—what his grandfather had learned about God. What reasons can you think of why some people follow the faith of their fathers and others don't? (See Joshua 24:15.)

_____

_____

_____

_____

_____

_____

_____

_____

_____

_____

_____

_____

_____

_____

Chapter 9
Text Messaging
(Daniel 5)

"He pinched me again."

That was the disturbing message that lit up on my iPhone as I headed home from some professional meetings. The phone number attached to the provocative text didn't come from my contact list, and I didn't recognize the area code.

I stared at my cell phone, and despite my best efforts to resist, a bunch of questions rushed through my mind.

Who is pinching?

Why are they pinching?

What are they pinching?

Dying from curiosity, I replied with a text of my own: "Who is this?"

The mystery texter responded hastily with a haunting missive that served only to surround this exchange with even more mystery: "Never mind—wrong number."

So I don't get to know about the pinching?

I guess I could have pressed the issue by pointing out the mental anguish such a text causes the recipient, and that while it may be easy for the *sender* to say "never mind," *I* desperately wanted to know just what was going on. It would have been merely a matter of politeness for the mystery person to provide me with the context of such a bizarre wrong message so I could sleep at night instead of lying awake, wondering what the cryptic text meant.

Then again, maybe I wouldn't want to know. Maybe it was really gross or stupid and would plague my brain with horrible images—which would be far worse than what I was going through then.

Whatever the case, it certainly isn't one of the ten worst texts ever received. Those positions of honor belong to other messages—such as the one Daniel 5 tells us Belshazzar got.

After King Nebuchadnezzar died, his grandson, Belshazzar, assumed the position of coruler of the kingdom of Babylon. When he's introduced in Daniel 5, he's holding a party for a whopping one thousand people. The most I have ever been allowed to invite to a get-together is twenty.

The text says that Belshazzar "drank wine in front of the thousand," and that when he "tasted the wine, [he] commanded that the vessels of gold and of silver which Nebuchadnezzar his father [a term that can mean *ancestor*—in this case, his grandfather] had taken out of the temple in Jerusalem be brought, that the king and his lords, his wives, and his concubines might drink from them" (Daniel 5:1–3).

Many people stress out regarding what kinds of dishes to use at various gatherings. My wife likes to use our wedding china for Sabbath meals on Friday nights and Saturday afternoons. It's important that the dishes reflect the occasion. You wouldn't use fine china at a birthday party for four-year-olds at a community swimming pool, and you wouldn't use paper plates when serving a formal meal at the White House— and you absolutely would never, ever, *ever* use holy utensils from God's sanctuary at your drunken booze fest—a spiritual faux pas Belshazzar learns about the hard way.

A creepy text message

Scripture says that not only did Belshazzar and his guests use the sacred dinnerware to get drunk, but they also "praised the gods of gold and silver, bronze, iron, wood, and stone" (verse 4). The partiers took God's goblets and made little idols out of them. Notice that Scripture lists the metals in the same order as they appear in Nebuchadnezzar's statue dream. Some people have interpreted this as indicating that Belshazzar was making fun of his grandfather's dream.

Sometimes people need strong reminders to mind their manners. God sent Belshazzar and his buddies a text message that ended the party. According to Scripture, "immediately the fingers of a man's hand appeared and wrote on the plaster of the wall of the king's palace, opposite the lampstand; and the king saw the hand as it wrote" (verse 5).

How's that for creepy?

It's one thing when someone hires a magician to entertain at a party, and the magician does a cool, floating-hand trick; but this floating hand was no trick. Its fingers etched something into the wall. Real. Tangible. No joke.

The effect wasn't lost on Belshazzar. "Then the king's color changed, and his thoughts alarmed him; his limbs gave way, and his knees knocked together" (verse 6).

The party's over.

The drunk has become sober—and scared spitless.

Cue the king's panic attack.

Immediately he calls for all the enchanters, wizards, wise men, witches, soothsayers, seers, astrologers, dragons, circus animals, talking parrots, and spelling bee champions to come and figure out what just happened. OK, so he didn't call for *all*

Study Question

What similarities do you see between Belshazzar's experience (Daniel 5) and his grandfather's (Daniel 2 and 4)?

_____

_____

_____

_____

_____

_____

_____

_____

_____

_____

_____

_____

_____

_____

_____

_____

_____

_____

_____

_____

_____

Study Question

of them, but he did send for the same ones his grandfather gathered after he had that nightmare (Daniel 2). Then he promised a reward to whoever figured out what's going on: "Whoever reads this writing, and shows me its interpretation, shall be clothed with purple, and have a chain of gold about his neck, and shall be the third ruler in the kingdom" (Daniel 5:7). Naturally, just as in his grandfather's story, no one could interpret the message.

The Bible says Belshazzar becomes alarmed and changes color again (maybe from a bright red to a pale white?). Fortunately, he has one relative who has a clue—his grandmother. "Because of the words of the king and his lords, [the queen] came into the banqueting hall; and . . . said, 'O king, live for ever! Let not your thoughts alarm you or your color change. There is in your kingdom a man in whom is the spirit of the holy gods' " (verses 10, 11).

Thanks, Grandma!

So, Grandma tells her grandson about Daniel—now an old man—who helped his "father [grandfather]" in days of old because Daniel has the "spirit of the holy gods" inside him.

Desperate to have the message deciphered, Belshazzar sends for Daniel. And when Daniel arrives, Belshazzar flatters him, and offers to make him the third in line in the kingdom, and gives him lots of cool, shiny, blingy things.

But Daniel isn't impressed. "Then Daniel answered before the king, 'Let your gifts be for yourself, and give your rewards to another; nevertheless I will read the writing to the king and make known to him the interpretation' " (verse 17).

Ouch.

With all the partygoers standing in awe, Daniel moves to the wall and begins to interpret what has been scrawled there. He talks about the greatness of Belshazzar's grandfather, Nebuchadnezzar, and how God blessed Babylon and made it powerful. Next, he tells the story of Nebuchadnezzar's life as an ox and how he humbled himself before the Lord. Then he drops the bomb.

> "And you his son, Belshazzar, have not humbled your heart, though you knew all this, but you have lifted up yourself against the Lord of heaven; and the vessels of his house have been brought in before you, and you and your lords, your wives, and your concubines have drunk wine from them; and you have praised the gods of silver and gold, of bronze, iron, wood, and stone, which do not see or hear or know, but the God in whose hand is your breath, and whose are all your ways, you have not honored" (verses 22, 23).

At this point it's probably safe to say that while Belshazzar doesn't know the precise meaning of the handwriting on the wall, he has a pretty good idea that the note from heaven is not a happy one.

Doomsday

Daniel then reads the text message, which consists of four Aramaic words, and he gives the meaning of each of the words:

- MENE, MENE: God has numbered the days of your kingdom.
- TEKEL: You have been weighed in the balances and found wanting (or lacking).
- PARSIN: Your kingdom is divided and given to the Medes and Persians.

True to his word, and against Daniel's wishes, the king clothes him with the cool, shiny, blingy stuff and makes him third in charge. But who wants to be in charge of a kingdom being ransacked, which is exactly what was happening at the time the text message came?

Too bad the partygoers were too tipsy to do anything about it. "That very night Belshazzar the Chaldean king was slain. And Darius the Mede received the kingdom, being about sixty-two years old" (verses 30, 31). In other words, you booze, you lose.

According to the prophetic dream given to Nebuchadnezzar, the kingdom of the Medes and Persians (a.k.a. the chest of silver) was to follow Babylon. In Daniel 5, we see prophecy fulfilled as Babylon and Belshazzar fall to Darius the Mede.

Babylon had seemed to be impregnable. At first, King Cyrus's general, Darius, couldn't find a weakness in its defenses. Then he came up with a plan. The mighty Euphrates River flowed through the city, which had gates over the river. Darius would lower the water level by having his troops dig a channel to divert the water into a nearby lakebed.

It worked! When the water level dropped, the troops ducked under the gates and marched into the city. The ancient historian Herodotus wrote, "The Babylonians themselves say that owing to the great size of the city the outskirts were captured without people in the centre knowing anything about it; there was a festival going on, and they continued to dance and enjoy themselves, until they learned the news the hard way. That, then, is the story of the first capture of Babylon."[1]

A party crashed, and a prophecy fulfilled.

CHAPTER 9 IN BRIEF

Galatians 6:7 says, "God is not mocked, for whatever a man sows, that he will also reap." Belshazzar flippantly took things sacred to God and used them for his own worthless ends. And he paid for it with his life. But some people persist in their stubbornness and arrogance, and eventually that catches up with them.

Bible prophecy hammers home the importance of worshiping the true

Belshazzar went to his grandmother for help when he didn't understand what was going on. Who can you go to when you need help in understanding God's Word?

Study Question

Belshazzar's party lifestyle led him to mistreat the sacred utensils that belonged to God's sanctuary (Daniel 5:2-4). What kinds of activities do people engage in today that can lead them to make fun of faith?

_____

_____

_____

_____

_____

_____

_____

_____

_____

_____

_____

_____

_____

_____

_____

_____

_____

_____

_____

_____

God and not dinnerware made from precious metals, not anything other than Him. It also demonstrates that God is a communicator. He sends dreams, visions, and even text messages to tell us what He's doing. He gives us numerous opportunities to humble ourselves and worship Him just as He gave Nebuchadnezzar. We study prophecy not only to learn God's plan for the future but also to remind ourselves that time belongs to God. He gives us time to align ourselves with Him before He moves to the next phase of His plan. And because He is a God of love, His heart aches for us to make the right decisions.

In this story, we also see that when it comes to serving God, age doesn't matter. Even when Daniel is an old man, the Spirit of God works in his life. Daniel remains unimpressed with everything that Belshazzar offers him and chooses to serve God, because who you decide to worship isn't a matter of who gives you the most goodies. As a result, while Babylon crumbles, Daniel's influence continues. And as the Medes and Persians step into their slot in prophetic history, Daniel continues to see things no one else does.

ENDNOTE

1. Herodotus, *Histories,* 1.190, 191.

Chapter 10
Deadly Decisions
(Daniel 6)

Study Question

Darius, the new ruler of Babylon, not only keeps Daniel on staff, but he promotes him. What reasons might Darius have had for keeping Daniel at his side?

"Don't lift it. Wait for me to help you."

My wife's words fell on deaf ears that morning as we packed to visit friends for Thanksgiving. After all, I am a *man*—a man with muscles that could certainly handle a box containing some puny shelves. We'd been keeping them for one of our friends after my wife helped her spend money at IKEA. This friend needed us to deliver them to her house because she didn't have an awesome minivan like we did—which, of course, made us the envy of all my friends, who drive wimpy sports cars and SUVs instead.

If we were going to deliver the shelves, they had to be loaded into the cavernous space of the van. This required muscles—which I have. Couple that with the facts that we were in a hurry and that on our last family trip my wife had chastised me for not being as helpful as I could have been, and you'll understand why I felt the need to display my epic strength by hoisting the shelves with my massive arms and placing them in our vehicle.

The box had a ridiculous warning printed on it. It pictured a man trying to lift the shelves by himself, and a bunch of sharp lightning bolts emanating from his back. People in their right minds would interpret this to mean that a person lifting the shelves without help could suffer an injury. However, I wasn't in my right mind that morning, so I took the symbol to mean that men who were as powerful as lightning could carry the box. So I grabbed the box, lifted it with lightning speed, carried it over to the van, and placed it inside. And I felt lightninglike pain shoot up my lower back.

At least my wife would be impressed by my, you know, "taking one for the team" so we could get a move on. When I told her what I'd done, she said, "Really? You lifted that all by yourself?"

"Yes," I said proudly, wincing at the pain. "Aren't you impressed?"

"No," she said crossly, seeing the discomfort I was suffering. "That was stupid. Now we'll have to pay for you to see the chiropractor."

Well, at least it gave me an illustration for this chapter. The point is that I made the decision to ignore a clear warning, and my decision caused me a great deal of pain. But I survived. Daniel 6 tells of several decisions people made in spite of clear warnings—and those decisions were fatal.

It's a trap!

The chapter opens up with Darius the Mede in charge of Babylon, having overthrown the brat Belshazzar (Daniel 5). He appoints some leaders to help him out: 120 princes and three presidents to supervise them.

Our man Daniel is one of those presidents (Daniel 6:1, 2). But he's a lightning rod. Not only is he in a position of tremendous authority in this new kingdom, but people like him more than they like the other presidents. So, jealousy ensues, and the other leaders try to get Daniel in trouble.

"Then the presidents and the satraps sought to find a ground for complaint against Daniel with regard to the kingdom; but they could find no ground for complaint or any fault, because he was faithful, and no error or fault was found in him. Then these men said, 'We shall not find any ground for complaint against this Daniel unless we find it in connection with the law of his God' " (verses 4, 5).

Daniel is such a good man that the only way his opponents can get him in trouble is to use something good that he does against him. So they decide to get the king to agree to outlaw all prayers directed to anyone but King Darius (verses 6–8).

Flattered by what he thinks is an honor, Darius decides to sign their proposal into law, not realizing that he has condemned his faithful servant Daniel to death. When he does, the officials leave the palace as giddy as a group of little girls at a princess tea party. They now have a document that condemns faithfulness to God. It is a clear legal warning, and Daniel knows all about it—which is what makes his next actions so crazy.

"*When Daniel knew that the document had been signed,* he went to his house where he had windows in his upper chamber open toward Jerusalem; and he got down upon his knees three times a day and prayed and gave thanks before his God, as he had done previously" (verse 10; emphasis added). Daniel flagrantly ignores the "warning label" and prays anyway—kind of like when I ignored the warning label on the box of shelves, except that I ignored the warning to glorify my own ego. Daniel ignored the man-made decree in order to honor God. He was making a statement.

Of course, the scheming politicians see him, and they break in and arrest him. Then, throwing Daniel before the king, they cry, " 'O king! Did you not sign an interdict, that any man who makes petition to any god or man within thirty days except to you, O king, shall be cast into the den of lions?' The king answered, 'The thing stands fast, according to the law of the Medes and Persians, which cannot be revoked' " (verse 12).

Then the schemers tell Darius that they've caught Daniel breaking the new law. The Bible says that then Darius "was much distressed, and set his mind to deliver Daniel; and he labored till the sun went down to rescue him" (verse 14). But eventually the king realizes there's nothing he can do. Daniel must keep his date with the lions.

Den of lions

The lion—commonly known as the king of the jungle—is four feet tall when it's down on all fours, and it weighs between three hundred and five hundred pounds. That's much larger than a house cat, in case you don't own pets and were wondering. The lion's mouth and paws are full of all kinds of pointy things, and it enjoys eating meat. Lots of meat. And lions aren't terribly particular about their meat diet either—they'll eat anything: elephants, each other, and, of course, tasty prophets if they can get their claws on them.

Gross.

So that the lions can catch that meat, their legs can propel them up to fifty miles an hour. Lions can also sleep up to twenty hours a day—which has nothing to do with this story but is worth mentioning because having a schedule that allows them to do that is really awesome!

Back to meat-eating: lions can consume up to seventy-five pounds of the stuff in one sitting. I have a friend who once ate a five-pound burrito. That's impressive, but not even close.

So, lions are beautiful, majestic creatures. And they're killing machines should the occasion arise—as journalist Charles Smith discovered in the fall of 2009.

Legends Resort in South Africa has a lion sanctuary on its premises. I've played with baby lions, so I can certainly appreciate people's desire to interact with them. It's no surprise that when Charles Smith had an opportunity to encounter a lion, he was all for it.

Mr. Smith was to "play" with a lion named Mapimpan, which means "little baby." All went well at first, but then "little baby" morphed into a little man-eater. Charles recounts his horrifying experience:

> [The lion] rose on to its haunches, towering above me and I was spun into a waltz with a 300 lb predator—as I pushed desperately at its throat to keep away its jaws. This did not feel like playing. . . . [The lion] was on me again, its teeth bared as it lunged towards my neck. I raised my forearm to divert its jaws from my face, then felt razor-sharp teeth ripping into my shoulder. The next few seconds were a blur of claws, teeth and shouts as I stumbled around, helpless against the power of this animal. . . . "They assume it's safe because

One commentator says that, according to tradition, Daniel's accusers would have questioned the authenticity of the miracle that occurred in the lions' den. They may have suggested that the king made sure the lions were so well fed that they weren't interested in munching on the prophet. But the king gave those jealous men the opportunity to see for themselves whether or not the lions were hungry (Daniel 6:23, 24). When is it OK to question God's miracles, and when is it best to just accept them by faith?

_____

_____

_____

_____

_____

_____

_____

_____

_____

_____

_____

Daniel's first response to the death decree was prayer. What do people typically do first when they encounter danger? What about Daniel's prayer life helped him to seek God in a time of stress? (Read Daniel 6:10.)

_____

_____

_____

_____

_____

_____

_____

_____

_____

_____

_____

_____

_____

_____

_____

_____

_____

_____

the ranger has a gun nearby," said Arrie [the sanctuary's lion expert]. "But they're wrong. The speed and power of the lion is quite phenomenal—they wouldn't stand a chance."[1]

Lions are not to be trifled with—and Daniel is about to be thrown into a den full of them.

And they're hungry.

As Daniel is escorted to the den of death, the king—grieving over the loss of his friend—declares, "May your God, whom you serve continually, deliver you!" (verse 16). Then "a stone was brought and laid upon the mouth of the den" (verse 17), sealing Daniel in and shutting the light out. Then, unless there were torches—and Scripture doesn't mention any—Daniel would have seen nothing. But I'm sure the smells and sounds made up for the loss of sight. Not only would there be leftovers from previous punishments strewn about the den, but after bingeing on seventy-five pounds of meat, I'm sure a lion has much to . . . uh . . . produce, if you know what I mean. The smell of death and of the other things left by the lions would have been overpowering. The ambiance of the place would have been conducive to fear and vomit, not hope and joy.

I've played tag in the dark and felt the excitement of knowing that any minute you could be caught. But to be in a pitch-black enclosure with a bunch of lions, to hear their breathing, the padding of their feet on the floor of the den, and their snarls would generate about the worst kind of excitement I can think of. When lions tag you, limbs go missing.

Darius was so upset that he couldn't sleep. No doubt the cruel officials who had tricked him into getting rid of Daniel either partied all night long to celebrate their victory or went home and slept peacefully.

When dawn broke, Darius ran to the den to see if anything remained of Daniel.

Caught in their own trap

There used to be a TV show called *America's Dumbest Criminals*. My favorite episode featured a crook who broke into a store by throwing a brick through a plate-glass window.

The proprietor of the store replaced the broken window with bullet-proof glass in case another criminal got the same idea. As a matter of fact, the *same* criminal got the same idea. He lobbed another brick at the store window, but instead of shattering the glass, the brick bounced back. And not only did it bounce back from the window, but it also bounced off the criminal's head, knocking him out cold, which made the police officers' job easy.

What does this story have to do with Daniel and Darius and the lions' den? Well, hang on just a minute.

The morning after Daniel was thrown to the lions, Darius races to the den, orders someone to roll the stone away, and shouts down into the den, "O Daniel, servant of the living God, has your God, whom you serve continually, been able to deliver you from the lions?" (verse 20).

Waiting for a reply was agony for Darius—but then a voice rose from the depths of the stinky lion pit. "Then Daniel said to the king, 'O king, live for ever! My God sent his angel and shut the lions' mouths, and they have not harmed me, because I was found blameless before him; and also before you, O king, I have done no wrong' " (verses 21, 22). And there was much rejoicing!

Darius praises God as Daniel emerges without so much as a scratch. And then Darius makes a couple more decisions. He decides to overturn the ridiculous law he signed the previous day, and he decides to feed someone else to the lions. "And the king commanded, and those men who had accused Daniel were brought and cast into the den of lions . . . and before they reached the bottom of the den the lions overpowered them and broke all their bones in pieces" (verse 24).

The decision to turn against God and His prophet despite all of the examples of His power that the officials in Babylon had seen proved to be a deadly mistake.

CHAPTER 10 IN BRIEF

All of us have been thrown into a den of lions of one sort or another. Before Daniel ever set foot into the lions' lair, he was surrounded by lions on the loose in the form of plotting politicians and coworkers who had jealousy issues. Sometimes people talk about us, make fun of us, and seek to do us harm. Even at work or at home, we can be stuck in the middle of prowling predators who want to take us down. But regardless of the power of those out to get us, God expects faithfulness.

Daniel knew the consequences of living his faith. By refusing to stop praying or to do his praying in secret, Daniel became a witness to the world that no lion—cat or human or circumstance—could keep him from worshiping his God. As a result, he faced lions. But God protected him. God promises to take a stand for all those who stand for Him—sometimes in this life, and if not then, at least when He returns to make the world new.

We also see again the danger of mixing religion and politics. By signing a decree regulating whom one could pray to, Darius inadvertently put a good friend's life in danger. We all have differences of opinion, and we can never force people to have faith in anyone. The only faith that counts is the one people choose freely, not because some law requires it or because someone makes them feel guilty if they don't believe their way.

Another important lesson we learn from Darius's mistake is simply that it's important to know what we're committing ourselves to. Had Darius taken the time to reflect on what his officials were asking him to sign, he might have

Study Question

What lions' dens do God's people face in today's world?

Notes

turned the whole thing down, making this chapter far less stressful for those involved. Just think of how many people have been hurt because they didn't get their facts straight when someone told them a story about "so and so" or forwarded them an e-mail full of wild claims.

Finally, this story demonstrates that our decisions have consequences, all the way from minor back pain to being fed to large cats. But our decisions can also be positive—we can ask for help to take a stand for God, who is able to protect us. Take the time to make good decisions so you can survive lions' dens without being digested.

ENDNOTE

1. Charles Starmer Smith, "Daily Telegraph Writer Mauled After Entering Lion's Enclosure," *Telegraph,* September 4, 2009, http://www.telegraph.co.uk/travel/travelnews /6139806/Daily-Telegraph-writer-mauled-after-entering-lions-enclosure.html.

Chapter 11
Animal Kingdoms
(Daniel 7)

Study Question

How has your picture of God grown clearer over the years?

_____

_____

_____

_____

_____

_____

_____

_____

_____

_____

_____

_____

_____

_____

_____

_____

_____

_____

_____

_____

_____

_____

_____

_____

_____

Animals make good symbols. Have you ever noticed how often we use them to represent other things? We have cars named Jaguar, Mustang, Rabbit, Ram, and Viper. Sports teams have animal names too: Bengals, Timberwolves, Ducks, Dolphins, Marlins, Panthers, and Falcons among them. Various schools of combat pattern modes of action after the tiger, the praying mantis, the crane, and even the monkey. We also use animals to describe people. We say things such as, "Stephanie is as quiet as a mouse"; "Ann is as mad as a hornet"; "Lucas is as slow as a turtle"; and "Travis is as big as a moose."

Even nations are symbolized by animals. The bald eagle is the symbol of the United States of America. In Russia, it's the bear; in Britain, it's the lion; and in Thailand, it's the elephant.

Bible prophecy frequently makes use of animals too. As we get into the prophecy recorded in Daniel 7, we'll see four beasts emerge from a stormy sea. What they symbolize reveals a lot about how God works in history.

In Daniel 7, our prophet moves from interpreting the dreams of other people to having dreams of his own. This happens when Nebuchadnezzar's bratty grandkid is the acting ruler of Babylon. The dream comes to Daniel during the night, and the first thing he sees is "the four winds of heaven," which are "stirring up the great sea" (verse 2). Not a good time to take the paddle boat out for a ride. Note that the winds come from heaven—meaning that despite the storm, God is in control.

In ancient times, the expression "the four winds" meant much the same thing as we mean when we refer to "the four points of the compass." Similarly, kings who wanted to impress people with the size of the territory they controlled would call themselves the rulers of "the four corners of the earth." In the Bible, the term often means the earth in its entirety (see Matthew 24:31).

As for the turbulent sea, in the book of Revelation—the Bible book most closely

It's interesting—and significant—that the prophecies progress from animals to horns plural to one little horn. This suggests that power over the world will move from large empires down into the hands of individuals. What are the implications of increasingly greater power becoming concentrated in the hands of fewer and fewer people—people who are opposed to God? What kind of power would you expect to see toward the end of world history?

_____

_____

_____

_____

_____

_____

_____

_____

_____

_____

related to Daniel—an angel explains, "The waters that you saw . . . are peoples and multitudes and nations and tongues" (Revelation 17:15). In Bible prophecy, then, bodies of water symbolize multitudes of people.

What's more, in the Bible, the sea and what dwells in it are consistently portrayed as representing those who struggle against God. "In that day the LORD with his hard and great and strong sword will punish Leviathan the fleeing serpent, Leviathan the twisting serpent, and he will slay the dragon that is in the sea" (Isaiah 27:1). "The wicked are like the tossing sea; for it cannot rest, and its waters toss up mire and dirt" (Isaiah 57:20).

So far, then, we see that Daniel's dream pictures the people of earth in turmoil, possibly set against God; but ultimately, God is directing what happens.

OK, now let's look at some animals.

Messed-up zoo animals

My daughter loves to go to the zoo. She takes weird delight in one particular corner of the animal kingdom. The part of the zoo that houses these animals is known as the Kingdoms of the Night; it's underground, dark, cavernous, cool, damp, and swampy.

Recently, a friend took my daughter and another little girl to the zoo. Upon their return, we received this report: "When we went to the Kingdoms of the Night, Aurora screamed and cried out, 'It's scary!' Maddie said, 'It's scary!' too, but she was smiling when she said it."

Two very different approaches to the underworld, where such cuddly critters as bats, bullfrogs, and lizards live.

I bet she gets it from her mother.

The animals in Daniel's dream are not the cute and cuddly variety you find in petting zoos. They would be right at home in the Kingdoms of the Night because, as you will see, they are, in fact, kingdoms of darkness.

In his dream, Daniel notices the bad weather and then sees "four great beasts [come] up out of the sea, different from one another" (Daniel 7:3). The angel who interprets Daniel's dream says, "These four great beasts are four kings who shall arise out of the earth" (verse 17). Four kingdoms arise from the turbulent peoples of the earth, each kingdom completely different from the others. Notice that the beasts parallel the four divisions of Nebuchadnezzar's nightmare statue of Daniel 2, representing the same kingdoms.

The flying lion. Daniel says the first beast "was like a lion and had eagles' wings. Then as I looked its wings were plucked off, and it was lifted up from the ground and made to stand upon two feet like a man; and the mind of a man was given to it" (verse 4).

Winged lions were common symbols in Mesopotamian dwellings, but in this case we aren't talking about wall decorations for someone's bedroom. In the Bible, wings often represent speed. The prophet Habakkuk described the Chaldeans this way: "Their horsemen come from afar; they *fly like an eagle swift to devour*" (Habakkuk 1:8; emphasis added). Psalm 18:10 says, "He rode on a cherub, and flew; he came swiftly upon the wings of the wind." And in Revelation we read, "they had scales like iron breastplates, and the noise of their wings was like the noise of many chariots with horses rushing into battle" (Revelation 9:9). Throughout Scripture, wings and flight are often used to represent great speed.

As for what the lion represents, the prophet Jeremiah helps us out. Jeremiah lived in the time when Daniel's people were taken captive, and he repeatedly warned them about Babylon. In one passage he says, "A lion has gone up from his thicket, a destroyer of nations has set out; he has gone forth from his place to make your land a waste; your cities will be ruins without inhabitant" (Jeremiah 4:7). And later on he states, "Israel is a hunted sheep driven away by lions. First the king of Assyria devoured him, and now at last Nebuchadnezzar king of Babylon has gnawed his bones" (Jeremiah 50:17). So, Daniel's prophetic pal Jeremiah likens Babylon to a lion.

Historical records show that the rulers of Babylon adopted the winged lion to represent their kingdom. Lions symbolized the Babylonian gods Marduk and Ishtar. Lion-eagle creatures also were used to denote an old story known as Bel and the Dragon.* This beast is clearly Babylonian.

The final clue comes in the picture of this animal standing up like a man. If you remember the strange little story in Daniel 4 about Babylon's king going wild like an animal and then being restored to his right mind, it should be apparent that this description is alluding to Nebuchadnezzar. The winged eagle who stands like a man represents the power of Babylon, which enabled it to conquer its enemies quickly. Unfortunately for this empire, its wings are plucked off, slowing it down until it was replaced by another power. And since we have looked at Daniel 2 and Nebuchadnezzar's nightmare, we already know the identification of the three beast kingdoms that follow Babylon on history's stage before the final act in which God's kingdom brings the play to a close.

The lopsided bear. "And behold, another beast, a second one, like a bear. It was raised up on one side; it had three ribs in its mouth between its teeth; and it was told, 'Arise, devour much flesh' " (Daniel 7:5). Even if this bear needs a chiropractor to help it with its lopsidedness, it still proves to be a scary specimen. Bears are usually hungry, which is why campers and tourists in bear country areas are told, "Don't feed the bears." In preparation for their winter naps, grizzly bears can gain up to four hundred pounds; that requires some intense eating! This prophetic bear enjoys its food too.

Based on our understanding of Daniel 2 and the identity of the previous winged

---

* Some translations of the book Daniel include this story, but most scholars don't consider it to be biblical.

3—P.D.M.S.

Study Questions

This vision occurs during the reign of the bratty Belshazzar, who for the most part ignored Daniel—a man who once was a trusted advisor to the king. Can the attitudes of people around us limit what we can do for God? Why, or why not? What can we do to avoid that? What should we do if we can't avoid it?

Notes

lion, we know this bear represents Media-Persia. The records of history point out that when the Medes conquered Babylon, the Persians were simply an ally, but in time the Persians took over leadership of the empire. This explains why one side of the bear is raised up higher than the other side.

As for the three ribs that the bear is munching, history suggests they represent the nations overthrown by Media-Persia: Lydia, Babylon, and Egypt. The Medes and Persians came down particularly hard on these three, moving some commentators to describe the conquerors as "cruel and rapacious, robbers and spoilers of the people."[1] Nice group.

The command to "rise and eat much flesh" makes sense because after these three powers fell, there was no stopping the bear kingdom from feeding on the lesser powers within its reach. Yet there is bad news for the bear—another kingdom rises. And as you will see in this card game of world kingdoms, four heads and four wings beat a raised side and three ribs.

The four-headed, four-winged leopard. "After this I looked, and lo, another, like a leopard, with four wings of a bird on its back; and the beast had four heads; and dominion was given to it" (verse 6).

Wow! Now there's something you don't see every day. You'd have a better chance locating a liger than finding this . . . thing. Looking back to Daniel 2, we know this power is Greece—but what of all the symbols?

If wings represent speed, then this kingdom moves twice as fast as the Babylonian winged lion. Comparing the two is like comparing an iPhone to a rotary phone, like comparing a Corvette to a bicycle. This kingdom conquers the world at blistering speed. Historical records point out that the Greek conqueror of the Medo-Persian Empire was Alexander the Great, whose conquests are spoken of as having no equal in the old world. By the age of thirty, he was already the creator of one of the largest empires of ancient times. (That's why his peeps called him "The Great," as in "Alexander the Great.") That's fast and impressive. Just think: you might be halfway to thirty, and all your empire consists of is a few electronics, unlimited texting, and a room in a house your parents own. Better get moving if you want to catch Alex.

As for the four heads, history reveals that after Alexander's death, his generals divided his kingdom, and each of them ruled the territory he acquired: Cassander had Macedonia and Greece; Lysimachus took Thrace and much of Asia Minor; Ptolemy ruled Egypt, Cyrenaica, and Palestine; and Seleucus claimed parts of Asia. Greece was epic and huge and fast, but despite its strengths, it couldn't match up with the final monster—a toothy, horned horror that terrorized the world.

The iron-toothed terror with horns. "After this I saw in the night visions, and behold, a fourth beast, terrible and dreadful and exceedingly strong; and it had great iron teeth; it devoured and broke in pieces, and stamped the residue with its feet. It was different from all the beasts that were before it; and it had ten horns" (verse 7).

What makes this critter so unnerving is that we really don't have much of a description of it. Some artists picture it like a dragon, but Daniel's description is limited to iron teeth, big feet, horns, and terror. It's a big, untamed creature with an appetite for destruction. However you picture this unique beast, the message is clear—it's more powerful than all the others. Again, based on Daniel 2, we know this power to be Rome—especially since Daniel 2 likens Rome to legs of iron, and this beast has iron teeth. As we noted in chapter 6, the army of the Roman Empire was known for its weapons—among them the iron spear called the *pilum*.

Rome's power had some good consequences. Since it crushed all opposition, the people who lived within the empire in the first and second centuries A.D. experienced the *Pax Romana*—the Roman Peace. Rome also broke new ground by developing advancements in military might, but also in politics and administration, which enabled it to rule for five hundred years—longer than any of the kingdoms that preceded it.

Now we could continue to nerd it up with all kinds of historical facts about the iron nature of Rome's power and might, and if you enjoying nerding it up, you can check out the books I've recommended in the back of this book. They'll tell you more about these empires. But for now we must move to the ten horns—especially the little one that, like the beast itself, has a big mouth.

CHAPTER 11 IN BRIEF

This chapter is a prophetic lens check on our understanding of the world powers introduced in Daniel 2. In this chapter, we are given clearer pictures of the nature and character of the powers that follow Babylon. The fourth beast, Rome, has a peculiar feature—the ten horns that grow out of its head, followed by a "little horn" that causes big problems (verses 7, 8). We'll study these horns in the next chapters of this book.

On a personal level, we can appreciate the fact that Bible prophecies about God's plans aren't just some vague platitudes and generalizations. When God tells us His plan of salvation and how it's going to affect life on earth, He reveals enough specifics so we can have confidence that the world isn't spinning out of control. These prophecies go over the same ground but with increasing detail. This tells us that God reveals His truth in ever brighter pictures. Daniel knew general details about the coming world powers, but as his relationship with God progressed, he saw even more clearly what God was doing in the world. God always has more that He can reveal—even about things we think we know well.

ENDNOTE

1. Smith, 108.

Study Questions

How do you have a discussion with someone who believes differently than you?

_____

_____

_____

_____

_____

_____

_____

How do you disagree without smothering the dialogue?

_____

_____

_____

_____

_____

_____

_____

_____

_____

_____

_____

Chapter 12
The Little Horn
(Daniel 7)

The potential for something to be grossly irritating and/or painful has little to do with its size. Consider the following physically puny entities and their ability to wreak havoc on everything good and decent.

Paper cuts	Artificial sweetener
Bullets	Germs
Hangnails	Viruses
Raindrops at an outdoor wedding	Words
Itches in the middle of your back	Sour notes
Mosquitoes that cause itches	Justin Bieber
Cavities	

As you can plainly see, the aforementioned list demonstrates that small things *can* cause monstrous amounts of damage physically, mentally, spiritually—and musically—to those who are near them.

The short but powerful Jedi Master Yoda once exclaimed, "Judge *me* by my size, do you?" to one of his students who was intimidated by a large task that loomed ahead of him. The point, of course, was that not everything that is big is powerful and not everything that is small is weak. And when we look at the next creature in the pantheon of prophetic symbols, it will become apparent that this little menace is the biggest pain in the entire book.

The little horn

After writing about the four beasts and the ten horns, Daniel continues with these words: "I considered the horns, and behold, there came up among them another horn, a little one" (Daniel 7:8).

To be honest, this chapter has been the most difficult to put together. The little horn is a big problem in prophecy and a big problem to write about. Everything the little horn does is big. It has a big mouth (verse 8), starts big fights (verse 21), becomes a big kingdom (verse 24), makes big changes because of big ambitions (verse 25), and then has a big fall (verse 26). And as if appearing in Daniel 7 weren't big enough, the greedy little horn pops up again in Daniel 8, where it becomes a big disruption (Daniel 8:11, 12) and a big liar (verse 25). If I hadn't condensed all the big hairy details of the little horn's big role in prophecy, this bulky chapter would bury you under a big bunch of details, causing your brain to explode. You don't want to experience such an occurrence.

Daniel 7 lists eight characteristics of the little horn:

1. The little horn came out of the fourth beast (verses 8, 24).
2. It comes *after* the "ten horns" (verse 24).
3. It appears little at first sight, but in time becomes "greater than its fellows" (verses 8, 20).
4. When it comes on the scene, the little horn uproots three other horns (verse 8).
5. It has "eyes like the eyes of a man" and a "mouth speaking great things" (verse 8).
6. It "shall wear out the saints of the Most High" (verse 25).
7. It tries to "change the times and the law" (verse 25).
8. It is given these crazy abilities for a "time, two times, and half a time" (verse 25).

So, who or what is the little horn? Part of the evidence that helps us to identify it comes from the text, and the rest comes from history.

As the vision unfolds, Daniel naturally wanted to know about "the horn which had eyes and a mouth that spoke great things, and which seemed greater than its fellows" (verse 20). Later in the chapter, the angel helping Daniel to understand the vision gives him (and us) a few details.

The angel lets Daniel know that "the fourth beast, . . . shall be a fourth kingdom on earth, which shall be different from all the kingdoms, and it shall devour the whole earth, and trample it down, and break it to pieces" (verse 23). In keeping with the prophecy in Daniel 2 and what we have discussed regarding the "animal" kingdoms in the previous chapter, you will remember that this "fourth beast" is Rome. The ten horns are ten kings who will arise from this kingdom of Rome (verse 24). Then the angel says the little horn is a kingdom that "shall arise after them [the ten horns]; . . . and shall put down three kings" (verse 24). After that, the angel simply lists the characteristics we looked at. So, all we really know at this point is that a little kingdom will make a big appearance and harass God's people and try to mess with God's truth—even making itself out to be on par with God Himself.

Instead of working our way through each characteristic and finding a historical application, I will tell you a brief historical story identifying this little creep and showing how it got so big. Within the story, I will set the prophetic descriptions in double quotation marks (even though in some places they aren't exact quotes).*

I must also tell you that while it may be tempting to write off history as a waste of time (which is what I did in high school), there's truth to the old adage that says "those who forget history are doomed to repeat it." Proverbs puts it a tad more crudely: "Like a dog that returns to his vomit, is a fool that repeats his folly" (Proverbs 26:11). In other words, if you don't understand history, you will do something stupid. In the case of our study, that means if you don't understand the little horn, you may put your own salvation in jeopardy.

The story of the little horn

Once upon a time, before all the churches on all the street corners in your town were built, only one church existed, and its name was Catholic, and its main base of operations was in Rome.

Catholic means "universal," and the name was appropriate: most Christians of the time agreed with the beliefs of the Catholic Church. To be sure, there were pockets of Christians who differed; but in the second and third centuries it was the Church in Rome that had the power. Sometimes that power was put to good use, such as the construction of universities and hospitals and the development of language. However, sometimes the power was used in a dark way, which I'll get to in a second.

Eventually, the Catholic Church became the Roman Catholic Church, due to the crumbling of the Roman Empire ("the fourth beast") because of the invasions of barbarian tribes into Rome's territory. Imagine trying to run a country in which scores of muscle-bound, pelt-clad, gnarly bearded wild men wielding swords, axes, and knives harassed and worse anyone they got their hands on.

The empire began to creak under these invasions, so the biased-toward-Christianity Emperor Constantine decided to skedaddle and move the capital city from Rome to Constantinople (now called Istanbul, which would make a great name for a cat).

The bishop of the Catholic Church in Rome had been the second most powerful man there, and the emperor's departure left him almost on his own, which increased his power. In the year 376, a horde of Visigoths (a barbarian tribe with beards) acquired permission to cross the river Danube into the Roman Empire. They came in waves, paddling canoes they had made by hollowing out tree trunks. (That has to be worth serious man points.) Their numbers were countless.

Over the next hundred years or so, the Visigoths were followed by bearded warriors from other tribes—most notably, the Ostrogoths, Vandals (the source of our term *vandalism*), Burgundians, Lombards, Anglo-Saxons, Franks (*not* the source of the synonym of "hot dogs"), the Alemannians, Heruls, and the Sueves. It is these

---

* I've borrowed this method from C. Mervyn Maxwell, although my telling of the story is far less professional.

barbarian tribes that make up Daniel's "ten horns."

Some of the ten tribes mentioned had been converted to Christianity before entering the Roman Empire, but their Christianity was not Catholic. Those who held their version of faith, known as Arianism, believed that Jesus, while really awesome, wasn't God. They believed God created Him an epic long time ago. The fact that the Catholic Church differed with them, teaching that Jesus is fully divine, created a little friction between the two groups—and by that I mean serious fights that involved kidnapping.

When the Arian Ostrogoths took over Italy in 493, they put some strong limits on the bishop of Rome in terms of power. The Ostrogoth king named Theodoric (also a good cat name) "bundled off" the Roman bishop—who was also called *pope* (which means "papa," or "father")—to Constantinople so he would quit pestering the Arians in what was left of the western part of the Roman Empire. A little while later he put the pope in jail, where he died.

Seeing all this go down, Rome's allies—the Catholic emperors who were now sticking pretty much to the eastern part of the empire—put the smack down on three tribes. Emperor Zeno (474–491) made a treaty with the Ostrogoths in 487 that resulted in the destruction of the kingdom of the Arian Heruls in 493. The Catholic emperor Justinian (527–534) broke down the Arian Vandals in 534, and then, in 538, those infernal Arian Ostrogoths (the pope-nappers).

The "plucking up by the roots" of the "three horns" represents the tearing down of the barbarian alliance (a cool name for an after-school club dedicated to making the community a safer place) of the Heruls, Vandals, and Ostrogoths. With those three out of the way, the Roman bishop—a.k.a. the pope—had the freedom to grow in power, slowly transforming the Catholic Church into the Roman Catholic Church.

Interlude: What time is it?

We're going to leave the pope basking in his growing power for a moment so we can address the issue of time. How many times have you asked about time? When we're struggling to wake up for work, we often ask, "What time is it?" in the vain hope that we still have ten precious minutes to sleep before being whisked away to another eight- to twelve-hour shift in the proverbial salt mines—unless you actually work in a salt mine.

We ask, "What time is it?" when church is crawling along at a sloth's pace, and we ask, "What time is it?" when we don't want to miss the season premiere or the finale of our favorite show. There are scores of other sensitive scenarios involving accurate time keeping: we want to know if there's still time for us to use the restroom before the flight departs the airport, we want to know about time when we're picking up the kids after school or when we're waiting for a ride to take us to the surprise party for Grandma.

And, of course, time matters when we're wondering how long the little twerp will be allowed to have such power over God's people.

The angel tells Daniel that the little horn will have "a time, two times, and half a time" to harass the "saints of the Most High" before his dominion is broken. Since

Study Questions

Fights about religion are always ugly. What makes them worse than physical fights? What kinds of things does your church fight about? How can people in a church disagree without getting into a nasty fight?

_____

_____

_____

_____

_____

_____

_____

_____

_____

_____

_____

_____

_____

_____

_____

_____

_____

_____

we don't use the expression "a time, two times, and half a time" to tell time nowadays, we need a little help.

When old Nebuchadnezzar had his "mind like a beast" incident in Daniel 4, Scripture says the punishment will last for "seven times" (verse 32), which scholars and linguists understand to mean seven years. And since one prophetic day represents one literal year, we consider the phrase "a time, two times, and half a time" to represent three and a half *prophetic* years—"time" meaning one year, "two times" meaning two years, and "half a time" meaning a half a year. At that time, the Jews allotted thirty days to each month, and since Daniel was a Jew, his year, unlike ours, consisted of 360 days. This means that if we multiply the 360 days per year by the three and a half years specified in the prophecy, we end up with 1,260 prophetic days. And since we've found that a prophetic day represents a literal year, 1,260 prophetic days must represent 1,260 literal years.

Yay math?

OK, so here's another way to look at the equation:

"A time, two times, and half a time" = 3.5 prophetic years

3.5 prophetic years = 1,260 prophetic days (because the Jews only had 360 days in their year)

1,260 prophetic days = 1,260 literal years

So, the angel is telling Daniel that the papal power will have its way for 1,260 years. And since the last of the three barbarian obstacles fell in 538 (bye-bye Ostrogoths), we add the 1,260 years to 538. That gives us the year 1798 as the time when the pope's "dominion" would end.

How did it end?

During the French Revolution, the French General Berthier (exceptional hamster name) received orders to arrest Pope Pius VI. A party was being held in the Sistine (not Sixteen) Chapel in Rome to celebrate his coming into power. Berthier crashed the party, pilfered Pius from it, and carried him into exile. Pius died in captivity, delivering a devastating blow to papal supremacy.

Welcome to your first prophetic timeline. You can practice drawing it. It looks like this:

Hastily Drawn Figure 12.1

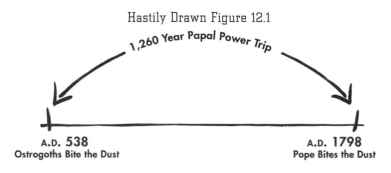

1,260 Year Papal Power Trip

A.D. **538**
Ostrogoths Bite the Dust

A.D. **1798**
Pope Bites the Dust

So, what did the "little horn"—a.k.a. the Roman Catholic Church—do for 1,260 years?

Back to the story.

Filling prophetic time with papal Rome

Without the barbarians who had opposed him, the pope emerged as the most prominent figure in the western Roman Empire ("greater than its fellows"). Think of *American Idol,* only set in Rome in the Middle Ages. The capital had been changed, distancing the heads of the civilian government and of the military, and the barbarians had been violently "voted off," so now the pope could develop political as well as religious power.

The fusion of political and religious power reached its peak in 1076, when Pope Gregory excommunicated King Henry IV and told his subjects that if Henry didn't repent of his sins, they didn't have to obey him. Even though Henry was the most powerful monarch (not the butterfly) in Europe, the pope had an ace in the card deck of authority. The church was viewed as the only road to salvation, and since the pope excommunicated Henry (no more church for you, buddy), it put the rebellious ruler in a bit of a pickle.

Out of the Catholic Church = no salvation.

Bummer.

Naturally, King Henry wanted to be in heaven. He also wanted all his people to follow him. (They, too, could lose their ticket to ride on the gospel train if they didn't follow the pope.) So, the king took a little excursion to the pope's winter palace at Canossa in the Alps. Far from being a winter vacation, this trip was a snow-laden, barefoot, freeze-your-heinie-off-in-hopes-of-forgiveness festival that lasted three frigid days.

Finally, the pope emerged from the palace and said Henry could come back to the church—and the answer to the question of who had more power became abundantly clear in the minds of all involved.

But perhaps more striking than these head-butting power struggles are the statements made in reference to the pope. In 1512, at the Fifth Lateran Council (which was like a prayer conference on steroids), Christopher Marcellus told Pope Julius II, "Thou art the Shepherd, thou art the Physician, thou art the Governor, thou art the Husbandman, finally, *thou art another God on earth.*"[1] Weirdly enough, Pope Jules no. 2 accepted the "compliment." But then, the little horn in Daniel's vision had a "mouth speaking great things." Maybe even more weirdly, this pope was known for his military leadership, not his gentle pastoral personality. (You're wondering whether his personality actually was gently pastoral?)

Not only did the Roman Church have great aspirations and great power, but as a religious system, it became a great bully toward anyone who didn't share its beliefs. Bullies are bad news at school, but they are even worse in political and religious

Notes

governing bodies—because bodies are exactly what begin to pile up.

Groups such as the Waldensians, Albigenses, and French Huguenots were invited to bonfire vespers that involved their actually being strapped to large wooden stakes *in* the bonfires. Estimates vary as to exactly how many people lost their lives because they didn't subscribe to Roman Catholic theology or recognize the pope's authority, but we can say that it was thousands. In fact, upwards of eight million people—Catholics as well as non-Catholics—died in a nasty conflict called the Thirty Years' War (1618–1648), which began chiefly over matters of religion.* These events, and others too horrible to mention confirm that this little-horn power "[wore] out the saints."

The last identifier we need to concern ourselves with is the little horn's "[thinking] to change the times and the law." Please note the word *thinking* in the description. Just because you think about doing something doesn't mean you do it. Many people think about exercise, homework, giving up smoking, or walking the dog, and some of them even give it a good try, but that doesn't mean they succeed. The little horn made a valiant attempt to alter God's law, and, in a way, it succeeded—even if only in the minds of lots of people, including people alive today.

On March 7, 321, A.D., Emperor Constantine passed a law that stated, "On the venerable day of the sun [Sunday, in other words] let magistrates and people residing in cities rest, and let all workshops be closed."

A mandatory day off? How can you argue with that? Because Christianity and paganism were learning to coexist in the now Holy Roman Empire (thanks to Constantine, who made Christianity legal instead of lethal), Sunday was chosen because it had meaning for both Christians (since Jesus rose on Sunday) and pagans (who worshiped the sun). It was a political law meant to unite the citizens of the empire. But as time went on, it took on religious overtones.

In the same year that the Ostrogoths got the boot, A.D. 538, the Catholic Church held the Third Council of Orleans (in France, not Louisiana). At this meeting, a statement known as the Twenty-eighth Canon found its way into church law. It says that on "Sunday[,] . . . agricultural labor ought to be laid aside, in order that people may not be prevented from attending church."

While that statement may seem pretty unthreatening, it carries the same tone as when my wife says, "I'd like you to take out the trash." That statement isn't a wish—it's a subtle command. I've learned this the hard way.

Sunday or Sabbath—who cares?

A mandatory day of worship might seem like a minor matter (like not brushing

---

* One of the reasons the war broke out has a name—the Second Defenestration of Prague. That's a fancy way of saying that a group of Protestants threw two Catholic officials out of a castle window. They survived because they landed in a pile of manure. Some Catholics later said the two officials survived because angels slowed their fall. Perhaps some thought the angels put the manure there.

your teeth), but a closer look reveals that its results are far more serious (halitosis, gingivitis, and tooth decay).

By the middle of the second century, the practice of observing Sunday as a day of worship in honor of the Resurrection was widespread. About A.D. 160, Justin Martyr said, "Sunday is the day on which we hold our common assembly"[2] (a.k.a. church). A number of arguments were made for worshiping on Sunday instead of Sabbath, one of the stronger ones being that by Jesus' day the Sabbath had become a tad crusty with all kinds of dos and don'ts—such as how far you could walk, how much you could carry, and even how often you could go to the bathroom. Christians wanted to distance themselves from that kind of legalism. In fact, they wanted to get rid of everything they could that connected them with the Jews because Rome and the Jews were at odds with each other—and it was obvious Rome was going to come out on top; it had already decimated Jerusalem and the Jewish temple.

However, while people in places such as Rome (Justin Martyr's hometown) and Alexandria (a city with a really cool library) began keeping Sunday holy, everyone else continued holding services on Sabbath. Christians in Egypt (pyramids), Turkey (not the bird), Palestine (hometown of lots of fighting), France (croissants), Italy (the Mario brothers), and more got their church time on day number seven instead of day number one. Conflict about the day of worship increased as Roman Catholicism's political and religious power grew and it tried its best to phase out Sabbath worship wherever it could. Not only did it exercise its influence, but it was sassy about it.

During the Protestant Reformation (in which Martin Luther and his peeps challenged the pope and his authority), a Catholic scholar named Johann Eck taunted Luther by saying, "Scripture teaches: 'Remember to hallow the Sabbath day; six days shall you labor and do all your work, but the seventh day is the Sabbath day of the Lord your God,' etc. Yet the church has changed the Sabbath into Sunday on its own authority, on which you [Luther] have no Scripture." What made this an incredible burn on Luther was that he prided himself on getting all his theology from the Bible and not from the church.

It seems everybody has trouble with consistency!

However, Scripture is consistent on the topic of the Sabbath, the day of worship; it always points to the seventh day. The Sabbath is the first thing Scripture says God made holy (Genesis 2:3). It is number four among the Ten Commandments (Exodus 20:11). Jesus kept it (Luke 4:16). It's more than a day; it's sacred time that God Himself established, so all those who tamper with it and try to reschedule are—by their actions—saying they think they have the same authority that God has—they're equal to God. But only God can change God's laws.

It's a shame that some people think otherwise—people such as Petrus de Ancharano, who in 1400 said, "The pope can modify divine law, since his power is not of man, but of God, and he acts in the place of God upon earth, with the fullest power of binding and loosing his sheep."[3] And then there's Gaspare de Fosso, archbishop of Reggio, who, at the Council of Trent in 1562, stated, "The Sabbath, the most glorious day in the law, has been changed into the Lord's Day [Sunday]. . . . These and other similar matters have not ceased by virtue of Christ's teaching, but they have been changed by the authority of the church."[4]

Daniel said the little horn would "think to change the times and the law." The Sabbath is a *law* about *time.* Unfortunately, while God's Sabbath is the seventh day of the week, people think that now, God's day is Sunday. This little switcheroo causes a major problem. It shows that something or someone wants to take God's place in your life and in the lives of everyone else on the planet. And it wants to do it in such a way as to make people think they are worshiping God when in reality they are following something else entirely.

Our salvation is dependent upon Jesus Christ; anything that replaces Him puts our salvation in jeopardy. We must not choose to place more stock in human-made rules and systems than in those that God has given us.

The truth of the Sabbath is multifaceted, but in this prophecy the issue at stake is the question of whose authority we follow: God's, or that of the little horn? Do we look to Scripture or to manmade tradition? Do we accept God's system of truth or that of human beings? The choice is ours—along with the consequences.

Do we hate Catholics?

Is the pope Protestant?

Nope.

Do we hate Catholics?

Nope again.

Roman Catholicism isn't portrayed positively in prophecy, but that doesn't mean Catholic people are mean, bad, and destined for the flames of judgment. Many sincere Catholics—including my grandparents—are firm believers in Jesus Christ as the Savior and are living examples of His love.

The apocalyptic angst of Daniel's prophecy is directed at the *system* that the Roman Church has become. Throughout history, the combination of politics and religion has resulted in dead bodies. That's true of Protestants too. In the early years of the United States, the general populace fused their Protestant roots with government, which resulted in—but was not limited to—the following destructive hobbies:

- Burning convents
- Making it illegal for Catholics to vote or hold property
- Writing scandalously false novels, such as *The Awful Disclosures of Maria Monk* and distributing them as the "truth" about what *really* went on between priests and nuns
- Destroying the homes of Catholic families

While the Roman Catholic Church is the historical fulfillment of Daniel's prophecy, the lesson is universally applicable for *all* religions: state-forced religion doesn't produce God-inspired faith.

CHAPTER 12 IN BRIEF

All the little horn's shenanigans can be summarized by saying that it is a religious system that sought to be more important than God and to establish its own ways to obtain salvation. When blended with political power, this system took the lives of thousands and led many other souls astray. By attempting to change God's law of the Sabbath, it sought to set itself over and above God and over the hearts of humans.

However, the spirit of the little horn isn't limited to Catholicism; it resides within every religious system—and within every heart. All of us are tempted to use force to get our perspectives across. Whether it's through mocking another faith, shunning those who differ from us, arguing chiefly to destroy other people's beliefs, or refusing to acknowledge that everyone has something positive to bring to the discussion of faith can make us morph into little horns just as easily as it did the Roman Church.

We can also become little horns by believing that we can obtain salvation because of who we are, what we believe, how good we are, or how much we know. The church in Rome didn't start out as a political power. First, it became enamored with its own importance, which is something we all fall into from time to time. Our only hope is the Person in whom we place our trust—namely, Jesus. He has the power to keep our little egos in check so they don't become big problems later on.

ENDNOTES

1. J. D. Mansi, ed., *Sacrorum Conciliorum nova et amplissima collectio,* 32:761.
2. Justin Martyr, "Weekly Worship of the Christians," chapter 67 in *The First Apology of Justin,* vol. 1 of *The Ante-Nicene Fathers,* 186.
3. Petrus de Ancharano, quoted in Lucius Ferraris, "Papa," article 2 in *Prompta Bibliotheca,* vol. 6 (Venice: Gaspar Storti, 1772), 29.
4. Gaspare de Fosso, quoted in Mansi, *Sacrorum Conciliorum,* 33:529, 530.

Notes

THE MADMAN:
A SHORT HISTORY

In the preceding chapter, we looked at the reasons many students of the Bible believe the little horn of prophecy represents the papal system—the Roman Catholic Church. Others, however, believe this prophetic figure represents someone else—a man who sicced his soldiers on the Jews, killing many, and who desecrated God's temple in Jerusalem, stopping the worship of God for several years. Could he be the little horn?

Human history contains a wide selection of disturbing little creatures. One such critter who made his deranged mark on the annals of time bore the name Antiochus IV (because apparently three wasn't enough). His friends called him "Antiochus Epiphanes." (I'm sure they loved learning to spell that.) His enemies called him something else: "Antiochus Epimanes"—"Antiochus the madman."

Antiochus got that nickname because of his ego, his bent toward killing people, and his sadistic sense of irony. In 167 B.C., he invaded Jerusalem on the Sabbath, knowing full well that the Jews wouldn't desecrate God's holy day by fighting. So, while the Jews did their best to keep their peace on this special day, Antiochus slaughtered them—men, women, and children.

When he had hacked and slashed his way through the defenseless population, he made his way to the Jewish temple. His ego demanded sacrifices. He ordered people to worship him as the god Zeus, and he had an idolatrous statue erected atop the altar in the temple. To make matters more disgusting, the madman got a pig—an animal the Jews considered spiritually unclean (they wouldn't even touch pigs), and had it slaughtered on the altar, defiling it.

Yuck.

This madman interrupted the Jews' sanctuary services for three years (168–165 B.C.) in such a revolting way that it inspired the Jews to revolt, and eventually they ousted him from their land. For these "gorrifying" reasons, many students of the Bible consider Antiochus IV Epiphanes to be the little horn spoken of in Daniel 7. However, there are good reasons to look elsewhere.

Why look elsewhere?

Antiochus Epiphanes is less than a good fit as the little horn for a number of reasons. First, horns represent kingdoms, not individual kings. Second, while people called Antiochus's father—Antiochus III, naturally—"the Great," they considered Antiochus IV flaky rather than admirable.

Third, Antiochus IV certainly hurt the Jews, but he managed to keep them under his thumb for only three years and ten days. Daniel 8, on the other hand, says the little-horn power will rule for 2,300 days, and even if you interpret those 2,300 days as regular, twenty-four-hour days, they amount to a longer period than Antiochus's tenure as king.

Fourth, Daniel 8:9 pictures the little horn as making impressive conquests. Antiochus did manage to make some headway in Egypt (to the south), but later, the Romans owned him, and eventually, he died in obscurity.

Finally, Antiochus reigned during the last days of the Greek Empire—which was the third of the four kingdoms pictured in Daniel's dreams. But in the prophecy, the little horn arises in the latter days of the *fourth* kingdom, which was centuries later; and it continues an active life right up to the judgment in earth's last days. Jesus indirectly confirms this point. Although His life on earth was long after Antiochus's day, He spoke of the "desolating sacrilege," a descriptive name of the little horn, as being still to come (Matthew 24:15; compare Daniel 8:13; 9:27).

So, while impressively disgusting, Antiochus doesn't fit Daniel's description of the little horn well enough to fulfill that prophecy. The real culprit is someone else—the papal system, as pointed out in the preceding chapter.

Compare the descriptions of Media-Persia and Greece in Daniel 8 to the descriptions of those two empires in Daniel 2 and 7. In what ways are they similar? In what ways do they differ?

Chapter 13
Showdown at the Ulai Canal
(Daniel 8:1–8)

People play flag football rather than tackle football for several reasons, a major one being to minimize injuries. However, every time I play flag football, someone walks away with a souvenir of the game in the form of a bruise, a dislocated finger, or something similar. My souvenir was a broken jaw.

When the ball was hiked on that fateful Sunday morning, all I could think about was making a catch. I had been only mildly productive for my team, and I really needed to make a catch and run it in for a touchdown to be happy with my performance. So I focused like a laser on the quarterback and the ball in his hand as I made a cut and ran swiftly across the field. What my focus was not . . . er . . . focusing on was my friend on the opposing team. He also had a laserlike focus on the ball, and he, too, had decided to make a cut and then race across the field at warp speed in order to intercept a pass, should the quarterback throw one.

Everyone on the field heard the collision. When a shoulder and a jaw collide, the jaw is the loser. A sickening *pop!* reverberated through my head, and I fell to the ground. When I rose to my hands and knees, three things caught my attention. First, some strange, raspberry-colored liquid was coming from my mouth, though, strangely enough, none of my teeth were missing. Second, I couldn't close my mouth. And third, I had the growing conviction that I needed to take a break from the game to go to the hospital.

My wife is amazing. She can perform daily duties while ill, stressed, tired, or in pain. In her humble opinion, in matters of illness or injury, men are babies when compared to women. So when I arrived home and said I needed her to take me to the emergency room, she agreed, though she was annoyed and thought I was overreacting.

After waiting for six hours in one of the most incompetent emergency rooms in the midwestern United States, I was X-rayed. As I lay in the room, barely able to talk understandably, the door opened and someone announced that I had a compound fracture of my jaw that required immediate surgery and a titanium plate.

Feeling vindicated, I garbled happily to my wife, "HEE? I TAHLD OO IDTH AWS BAHD!" My triumph was short lived though, ending when a nurse gave me a shot of penicillin in the rear to prevent infection.

Collisions can be incredibly violent. In the vision recorded in chapter 8, Daniel sees an epic one in which a pair of big horns is broken.

The setting

Daniel receives the vision of Daniel 8 two years after he had the vision recorded in chapter 7. Belshazzar is enjoying his third year as king—and being a royal pain. If you remember, Belshazzar's granddad was a gentleman and a scholar, but his bratty grandson loved to booze it up and hold wild parties. Daniel is serving this boneheaded king when a vision transports him to the Ulai Canal, which is located in Susa in the province of Elam (Daniel 8:1–3).

Where are these places? Susa became the winter capital city of the Medo-Persian kingdom after the Medes and Persians deposed Belshazzar. At the time of this vision, 551 B.C., Babylon would exist as an empire for only another twelve years till it fell to Darius, one of Cyrus's generals, during one of boozy Belshazzar's parties. By taking Daniel in vision to Susa, God foreshadowed what would happen when the current kingdom collapsed. God is about to adjust our prophetic lens again. The vision of Daniel 8 is a continuation of the ones in chapters 2 and 7. Like them, it picks up the theme of the succession of kingdoms through history.

This chapter has two parts: (1) the vision and (2) the interpretation of the vision given by the angel Gabriel. Understanding a symbolic vision is always easier when an angel shows up to tell us what's going down!

Ram and goat collide

"I looked up and saw a ram standing beside the river. It had two horns. Both horns were long, but one was longer than the other, and the longer one came up second. I saw the ram charging westward and northward and southward. All beasts were powerless to withstand it, and no one could rescue from its power; it did as it pleased and became strong" (Daniel 8:3, 4, NRSV).

This ram means business. He becomes strong and appears to be unstoppable. But while Daniel watches the ram, a goat comes onstage—one that grows "exceedingly great" (NRSV). What follows reminds me of what happens on some of the nature programs on television. Just as my little girl and I are watching the cute little deer that's snuffling flowers in a field, some random bear charges out of the woods and mauls it in high definition, leaving me to explain the grotesque atrocity to my daughter . . . and to pay for years of therapy.

Daniel says,

Study Question

Before you read the next chapter of this book, read Leviticus 16 and then list three major themes found in Leviticus 16.

Study Questions

What correlation do you see between the animals in the vision of Daniel 8 and the animals sacrificed on the Day of Atonement? What's the significance of the correlation? What reason do you think God might have had for using these animals in the vision of Daniel 8?

As I was watching, a male goat appeared from the west, coming across the face of the whole earth without touching the ground. The goat had a horn between its eyes. It came toward the ram with the two horns that I had seen standing beside the river, and it ran at it with savage force. I saw it approaching the ram. It was enraged against it and struck the ram, breaking its two horns. The ram did not have power to withstand it; it threw the ram down to the ground and trampled upon it, and there was no one who could rescue the ram from its power. Then the male goat grew exceedingly great (verses 5–8a, NRSV).

My experience with goats has been with the cute little pygmy variety found at petting zoos and some summer camps. They are sweet little things that let you feed and pet them. The wild, one-horned goat in this prophecy, however, wouldn't be allowed anywhere near a petting zoo, and probably wouldn't enjoy being petted anyway.

It runs so fast that its feet don't touch the ground until it rams the ram. The collision, which brings back painful memories of my own collision in that flag football game, breaks both of the ram's horns. And then, as if fracturing the horns weren't enough, the goat stomps all over the ram. Charming.

Scripture pictures this great, gloating goat standing over the trampled ram and then it says that at the height of the goat's power, "the great horn was broken, and in its place there came up four prominent horns toward the four winds of heaven" (verse 8b, NRSV). This should bring back memories of Daniel 7's four-headed beast, but just in case it doesn't, the angel Gabriel shows up and delivers to Daniel the interpretation of the vision of chapter 8.

Gabriel gives the answer

"When I, Daniel, had seen the vision, I sought to understand it; and behold, there stood before me one having the appearance of a man. And I heard a man's voice between the banks of the Ulai, and it called, 'Gabriel, make this man understand the vision.' So he came near where I stood; and when he came, I was frightened and fell upon my face. But he said to me, 'Understand, O son of man, that the vision is for the time of the end' " (verses 15–17).

So, right off the bat, we know this vision is about the future; we know that it extends right down to the "time of the end"—to the close of earth's history.

The angelic explanation continues in the next verses. "As for the ram which you saw with the two horns, these are the kings of Media and Persia. And the he-goat is the king of Greece; and the great horn between his eyes is the first king. As for the horn that was broken, in place of which four others arose, four kingdoms shall arise from his nation, but not with his power" (verses 20–22).

Media-Persia, the ram

Babylon is the first kingdom to appear in both Daniel 2 and 7. Chapter 8, however, begins with the kingdom that will defeat Babylon. The imagery in this vision is interesting because history shows that Media-Persia's coins featured a ram. History also tells us that Persian kings were crowned with a ram's head made of solid gold and encrusted with jewels. True, you might get harassed for wearing a headpiece like that now, but it's still an interesting historical fact with which the vision corresponds.

As we already saw in previous visions, this kingdom had two parts. King Cyrus made sure that the Persian part had more power—which matches what the prophecy points out: that one horn would rise above the other.

History also confirms the conquests this kingdom made. The prophecy says this power charged west, north, and south, and records do show that Media-Persia took over Babylonia, Syria, and Mesopotamia (west); Armenia and the region near the Caspian Sea (north); and Egypt, the Holy Land, Libya, and Ethiopia (south).

The goat of Greece

The goat that galloped a gazillion miles an hour is Greece. This picture of Greece matches the four-winged leopard in Daniel 7, which represented the speedy Greeks and their military might. The "great horn" is the "first king," Alexander the Great, who, as the prophecy pointed out, speedily defeated the other powers of the day.

The Hebrew term translated as "first" doesn't necessarily mean first in sequence. It can also mean "strongest" or "most important." No one in Greek history rivals Alexander the Great. He was an incredible warrior—once, with his cavalry, he chased some opposing forces almost continuously for three days and four nights. According to one story, at the battle of Arbela, the Medo-Persians outnumbered the Greeks one million to forty-seven thousand. How would you like those odds? On paper, the idea that the Greeks had a chance looks ridiculous; but we know that God has a plan, and He's in charge.

The Bible says that despite the numbers at play in that battle, the Greek goat would destroy the Medo-Persian ram. And history tells us that Darius, the ruler of the Medo-Persians at the time, lost his nerve and fled the battlefield three times. (This wasn't the Darius who captured the city of Babylon and who then learned the power of Daniel's God at the lions' den.) What happened to Darius's courage? Scripture says, "The king's heart is a stream of water in the hand of the LORD; he turns it wherever he will" (Proverbs 21:1). God can move the hearts of kings, and He can stop them when He determines that it's time to do so.

Daniel continues the story: "when he [Alexander] was strong, the great horn was broken, and instead of it there came up four conspicuous horns toward the four winds of heaven" (Daniel 8:8). Alexander had conquered everything within reach by the time he turned thirty-three—and then he died. Several theories have been put forward to explain what happened. One is that due to a drinking binge after a close friend's death, he, too, suffered the fate of Belshazzar—"You booze, you lose." Others speculate that Alexander's drinking habits made him susceptible to a fatal illness.

The vision says, "when he was strong, the great horn was broken, and instead of it there came up four conspicuous horns toward the four winds of heaven" (verse 8). From our discussion in chapter 7, we know that the four horns that arose after Alexander "was broken" were the "four kingdoms" that arose "from his nation" (Daniel 8:8, 22).

CHAPTER 13 IN BRIEF

Through another vision, God continued to show Daniel that He is directing history according to His plan. And when the vision ended, God sent an angel to give the interpretation to Daniel (and to us)—proving once again that Scripture interprets Scripture. Babylon was on the brink of fading away, so it wasn't included in any of the prophetic imagery. Daniel saw the Medo-Persian Empire duke it out with the Greek Empire and fall to it. Then the amazing Alexander the Great dies abruptly, and the Greek kingdom is divided into four parts.

This section of Daniel 8 offers us the assurance that even the most powerful forces on earth are subject to God. They can do only what God allows. So when you feel overpowered by foes or circumstances or you're concerned because of calamities happening in various parts of the world, remember that while for a time God allows evil to charge around in all directions, He will ultimately bring it to an end.

Chapter 14
Church Interrupted: The Little Horn Returns

(Daniel 8:9–27)

Study Question

Persecution is an unfortunate by-product of following God (see John 16:33). How can we stay strong during times of harassment?

It goes without saying that having random children run at you with reckless abandon while you're trying to preach can be a tad unsettling.

There I was, calmly expounding upon the Word of God, when lo and behold, a boy of two near the back of the church tumbled out of a pew into the center aisle, rose to his feet, and ran wildly in my direction. I thought, *Surely his mother will grab him.* But alas, she didn't seem interested in chasing him down.

I did my best to focus on the message, but I, along with everyone else, was distracted by the sprinting toddler. *What will he do when he reaches me?* I wondered. Then, just before the little freight train collided with me, a hand darted out from a pew and snatched him out of the center aisle. My parishioners and I breathed a sigh of relief and returned our focus to the church service.

Church disruptions come in a variety of exciting flavors. In addition to the runaway toddlers, there are the screamers. The shrieks of these babies hurt everyone's ears—except those of their parents. For some reason—maybe due to their constant exposure to the noise—their parents can't hear them. So, everyone else who wants to benefit from the service has to work at ignoring the pain.

Then you have the challengers. They're adults—people who don't follow the biblical counsel to talk one-on-one with those who offend them or who they believe are headed down the wrong track. That includes the preacher. The challengers prefer to stand up midservice and argue with the preacher in front of everyone. They want to take it to the people! What they take to the people isn't a well-executed argument against the speaker's message, but rather an epic time of uncomfortableness until the challenger is magically whisked off the church premises by several strong deacons.

Disruptions come in all kinds of forms, among them microphone squeals, text messages from friends, "special" music in which the singer *a-a-a-l-l-l-most* hits the right notes, and ill-conceived sermon illustrations, such as the preacher's describing child-birth in gross detail (very gross detail) during a Christmas sermon about Mary giving birth to Jesus in a stable. Then there's the exasperating little horn, who reappears in Daniel 8. He intends to interrupt our worship, too, by disrupting the services in God's sanctuary, changing God's laws, forcing people to worship his way, and stealing Jesus' job—a job that you and I depend on every day. We'll examine the little horn's attempts to interrupt the services in the sanctuary in heaven, but before we do that, we need to perform a background check on the little offender to be sure we have the guilty party.

Background Check 1: The little horn came from the west. Scripture says this little horn arises out of one of the four winds of heaven (Daniel 8:8, 9)—in other words, the four primary directions on a compass. (If you don't know what they are, I suggest that you invest in a GPS and avoid traveling far from civilization.) Verse 9 then informs us that the little horn grew exceedingly great toward the south, toward the east, and toward the "glorious land"—toward Palestine, in other words (see Ezekiel 20:6).

So, did Rome come from the north or from the west?

Rome did grow northward and westward—in other words, from the south and from the east. But Bible scholars point out that by 63 B.C. it had conquered lands to its south (Egypt), its east (Greece), and its southeast (Palestine). So, yes, from the perspective of the lands that are the primary concern of biblical prophecy, particularly apocalyptic prophecy, Rome came from the north and west.

Who cares? Why is this important?

It's important because when we can check what the Bible says with history and we find that history supports the biblical portrayal, our faith in the Bible grows. By telling us the *direction* from which Rome came (from the west), *when* the little horn would arrive on the scene (Daniel 8:23 says it would follow—timewise—the Greek kingdom, which fits nicely with the prophecies of Daniel 2 and 7), and *what* it would do (it started small and grew large enough, eventually, to take the place of the pagan Roman Empire), Scripture establishes itself as an accurate guide. One we can trust. Even in little things.

Background Check 2: The little horn has a history of violence directed against God's people. The picture in Bible prophecy of Rome's violent behavior begins with the little horn magnifying itself against the Prince of the host ("host" meaning the multitude of heavenly beings, not someone who greets you at a restaurant and takes you to your table). Jesus is the Prince of the host, and tragically, in A.D. 31, the pagan Roman Empire condemned Jesus to death by crucifixion. Scripture has four accounts (Matthew, Mark, Luke, and John) of Pontius Pilate (not "pilot"; airplanes hadn't been invented yet), the Roman governor of Judea, condemning Jesus to death, and Roman soldiers crucifying Him.

In the process, Pilate brought Jesus before a mob that was anxious to see Him dead, and when the crowd rejected Pilate's offer to pardon Him, Pilate had Him flogged (John 19:1). Being flogged meant being struck repeatedly with a whip made of strips of leather to which sharp pieces of metal and bone were attached. That whip could peel the flesh off a person's back. Many people who were worked over by a skilled flogger didn't survive. Jesus did.

Next, the soldiers placed a crown of thorns on Jesus' head and a purple robe on His bleeding back and shoulders, and they hit Him and mocked Him (verses 1–3). When they tired of that, they crucified Him—one of the most diabolically torturous forms of capital punishment.

And the violence continued even after Jesus died. The little horn sought to destroy the people who believed in Jesus, people whom Scripture calls saints (Daniel 8:24). Both pagan *and* Christian Rome took the lives of many dedicated believers. Pagan Rome beheaded James the son of Zebedee, crucified Simon Peter, and beheaded the apostle Paul. Christian Rome took followers of Jesus such as John Huss (who told the church to stop selling "indulgences," which the church was advertising as God's forgiveness for most any sin, as long as you paid the price) and Jerome of Prague (who followed John Huss) and burned them at the stake. These are but a tragic sampling of the lives lost when Christian believers stood in the way of Rome.

What we see so far points to Rome as the power represented by the little horn, just as we saw back in chapter 12. But in at least one way, the little horn of Daniel 8 differs from the little horn of Daniel 7. In Daniel 7, the prophet sees four beasts, which represent four empires, the fourth being the Roman Empire. In this vision, the little horn represents just the "Christianized" Roman Empire.

In chapter 8, on the other hand, while Daniel sees animals that represent Media-Persia and Greece, he doesn't see any that represent Rome. But chapter 8's description of the little horn shows that it has the attitude and does the things that make it an appropriate symbol for *both* pagan and papal Rome. That fits the case, because papal Rome eventually took over pagan Rome's place and carried on its activities. And as was true of Daniel 7, the primary concern of Daniel 8 is papal Rome—what it is and what it does.

Scripture says that as the saints fell, Christian Rome (the little horn) grew great even to the host of heaven (Daniel 8:10), even to the point of challenging the Prince of the host (verse 11). And "by his cunning he shall make deceit prosper under his hand. . . . Without warning he shall destroy many" (verse 25).

The little horn wants to interrupt Sabbath keeping and the sanctuary services.

A few years ago, several feet of snow fell all over my town. By Sabbath morning, six-foot drifts and too few snowplows made it impossible to go anywhere. Therefore, as the pastor, I had no choice but to cancel the church service. (Naturally, I used the day off constructively—another church member and I built a giant igloo in my front yard, one that could accommodate two adult men and my ninety-pound dog Winston. Neighbors took pictures, and I felt an incredible sense of pride at my exceptional architectural design.)

The little horn wanted to interrupt Sabbath services. In addition, Daniel 8:11

Study Questions

Many people view the concept of an investigative judgment (Jesus checking His books before He returns) as something scary. What would make it scary? In what way could it be comforting? How does Daniel 7:22 affect your picture of Jesus as Judge?

_____

_____

_____

_____

_____

_____

_____

_____

_____

_____

_____

_____

_____

_____

_____

says it would take away the "continual." Many translations render the Hebrew word as "daily" or "regular" instead of "continual" and then add "burnt offering," but that makes its meaning too narrow. The word translated "continual" touches on much more than just the burnt offerings.

When I studied Hebrew in college, I had class at seven-thirty in the morning. That's a rough time for anyone to begin classes, but it's especially hard when you're bleary-eyed from studying late the night before, and you're trying to learn a language (Hebrew) whose letters don't look anything like ours: the vowels are little dots and dashes under the consonants, which come in groups of ones, twos, and threes and sometimes randomly disappear for no explainable reason in some conjugations of the word. And on top of all that, the text reads from right to left instead of from left to right. It took a great deal of effort for me to uncross my eyes and focus them, and I had to struggle to resist the temptation to play connect-the-dots with the vowel pointing and to make little animals out of the Hebrew "characters" (letters).

I did pass the class, however, and one of the little Hebrew words I learned is תָּמִיד (*tamid,* in case you don't read Hebrew and are looking for a great nickname for your sister, who will have no idea what you are calling her—unless she reads this book). It's this little word that means "continual," and in the Bible, it is used in connection with *all* the services performed in the Old Testament sanctuary. Observe the following:

- *Tamid* refers to the continual offering of lambs—offerings made every morning and evening (Numbers 28:3).
- *Tamid* refers to keeping the sanctuary lamps burning continually (Leviticus 24:2).
- *Tamid* refers to the continual offering of showbread (2 Chronicles 2:4).
- *Tamid* refers to the breastplate that was adorned with jewels and continually worn by the high priest (Exodus 28:29, 30).
- *Tamid* refers to the burnt offerings mentioned in 2 Chronicles 24:14 as well as to the sacrifices offered on the sabbaths, new moons, and feast days (1 Chronicles 23:31).

So *tamid* refers to just about everything in the Old Testament sanctuary— hurray for *tamid!* But seriously, who cares?

The point, my dangerously-close-to-becoming-distracted friend, is that the little horn isn't interested in getting one part of God's sanctuary service, it wants the whole tamale.

Daniel 8:11 also says the little horn would overthrow the place of the sanctuary.

How does anyone mess up God's sanctuary?

The little horn used fire.

In A.D. 70, pagan Rome and the Jews in Jerusalem were as compatible as rusty nails and bare feet—and the Jews, or at least many of them, were the rusty nails.

They rebelled against their Roman overlords. Of course, the Romans were too powerful for the Jewish rebels and soon had the last of them under siege in Jerusalem. The Roman general Titus had given specific instructions that his soldiers were to spare the temple, which was one of the most beautiful buildings in the whole Roman Empire, but when the Roman army broke into Jerusalem, one of the soldiers threw a torch into the temple, where many Jews had sought refuge, and the temple was reduced to ash and memory.

Burning the temple was like burning the White House or London's Buckingham Palace. The temple was the cultural as well as the religious epicenter for the Jews, and watching it vanish in flames must have caused them unspeakable pain. Without it, they had nowhere to offer sacrifices; nowhere to get forgiveness for their sins.

However, the destruction of the center of the worship of God here on earth wasn't enough to satisfy the little horn. It wants to neutralize Jesus' ministry for us in the real center of our worship—the sanctuary or temple in heaven.

A tale of two priesthoods

The Bible tells us that the earthly sanctuary was modeled after the one in heaven (Hebrews 9:23), and that now, Jesus Christ ministers there as our High Priest (Hebrews 4:14). Everything in the Old Testament sanctuary pointed toward the heavenly sanctuary and the ministry of Jesus after His resurrection and ascension into heaven. Since Daniel's vision pictured the distant future (Daniel 8:24), we can conclude that it was picturing Christ's heavenly ministry, not the earthly ministry of human priests as described in the Old Testament. The little horn wants to unseat the Son of God, and in order to pull that off, it had to create another priesthood to replace Christ's—at least in people's minds.

I once watched a weird (and pretty awesome) Japanese game show that specialized in creating obstacles for contestants that bordered on the criminally dangerous. For example, one show featured a series of walls, each of which had several doors. The idea was for the contestant—who was being chased by people in giant monster and alien costumes (don't judge me; I already admitted it was weird)—to run full blast into the real door, which then would open, allowing the contestant to proceed to the next wall and set of doors.

The funniest parts of the show occurred when contestants threw themselves into the fake doors, which wouldn't open. *BOOM!* They went reeling backward into the arms of one of the costumed creatures—and as a consolation prize, brought home a headache (and possibly whiplash or paralysis, depending on the angle of their collision).

The little horn sets up a false priesthood, claiming that it is the "door" to salvation—when in fact it leads to a painful dead end.

Remember, I'm not claiming there are no followers of Jesus within Roman Catholicism. What I am saying is that Roman Catholicism has effectively replaced Christ's ministry as High Priest with human effort, tradition, and authority. As the

The Bible refers to our bodies as 'temples' (see 1 Corinthians 6:19). Some people believe that Jesus' work of cleansing the temple in heaven is related to sin being cleansed from our lives on earth. What do you think?

_____

_____

_____

_____

_____

_____

_____

_____

_____

_____

_____

_____

_____

_____

_____

_____

_____

Roman Church grew in power, it crafted a theological package that places people in spiritual peril.

The Baltimore Catechism contains Catholicism's doctrines as formulated at the Council of Trent (an important series of meetings lasting eight years in which the Catholic Church tried to combat the teaching of Martin Luther, who started the Protestant Reformation). The key teachings recorded in the Baltimore Catechism are as follows:

- To obtain forgiveness, people have to confess their sins to a human priest (sections 384, 408).
- The emblems of the Lord's Supper (a.k.a. Communion)—the bread and wine—actually become the body and blood of Jesus as the priest performs the service known as the Mass (sections 350, 359, 360).
- Special services can be held for souls in "purgatory" to reduce the suffering they must endure to be qualified to enter heaven (sections 137, 148, 162).
- The pope is the "supreme head" of the church (sections 137, 148, 162).

Part of the problem is that the Catholic Church teaches that it can never be wrong. The Baltimore Catechism says, "It is unthinkable that an institution established by God for the salvation of souls could lead men into error" (section 163). As we saw earlier in regard to the Sabbath, the Catholic Church claims to have authority over Scripture and to have the final word as to what it means.

The problem with the papal priesthood is that it nullifies what the Bible says Christ's role is in heaven. Scripture says the following:

- We can confess our sins *directly* to Jesus Christ (1 Peter 2:9; 1 Timothy 2:5).
- Jesus died "once and for all" (Hebrews 9:12), and the idea that any human being can call Jesus down so that His body and blood are present in the Communion service not only flies in the face of a risen Savior but also implies that human beings can control the heavenly High Priest.
- The pope isn't the head of the church; Jesus Christ is (Ephesians 4:15; 5:23).
- By creating doctrines like purgatory (with its corresponding "get out of purgatory" services—for a small fee), and, as we have discussed previously, by making the church the source of grace and forgiveness, Rome replaces Jesus as Judge (2 Timothy 4:1) and hides the reality that salvation and grace are obtained through faith (Ephesians 2:8) and are a free gift from Jesus (Romans 6:23).

Throughout the centuries and in the minds of millions today, the little horn has substituted an earthly priesthood for Christ's ministry in heaven. And despite what that system says, without Christ's ministry, we have no one to intercede for us and give us the grace and forgiveness we need.

Am I sure we don't hate Catholics? Is the pope Catholic?

Remember, the little horn is a symbol that, while certainly applicable to the office of the pope, also applies broadly to the whole Roman system of religion. God loves Catholics, many of whom are sincere and love Jesus and look to Him for salvation despite what their church teaches.

Good intentions, but faulty beliefs

The idea that to be forgiven we must confess our sins to a human priest developed in A.D. 250. Several church members had *apostatized* (adopted beliefs that differed from the church's understanding), and a small group of church leaders said their sin was so bad that they couldn't be forgiven. Other church leaders tried to help them out by saying that if they just confessed their sins to them as a demonstration of how sorry they were, they could come back into the church. Since no one likes to admit to other people that they were wrong (like that time I—never mind), they figured this would help people to take sin more seriously.

People were even burned at the stake in order to force them to confess their sins. The idea was that if the victims confessed, though their bodies were burned, their souls would go to heaven. So, the church was doing these "sinners" a favor by burning them at the stake. How thoughtful!

The point is that while we disagree with many of the doctrines of the Catholic Church, some of which even make us gasp in horror, the people who originated them may have had good intentions. However, we must always look to the Bible as our guide to truth, and not just what seems to be convenient or practical or helpful. Moreover, we need to remember that it's easier to look back and say, "That was dumb," than it is to come up with the right answer in the middle of a delicate situation. This means that we can disagree with what people did in the past and even shake our heads at it, while remaining humble because we realize that we may not have done any better in the same situation.

"Are we there yet?"

My parents owned a large conversion van that they used to contain their children's nonsense on long trips. In addition to miscellaneous noises, smells, and even fistfights, my siblings and I had an exceptional arsenal of annoying questions that heightened our parents' already boiling road rage. Among them was the great-granddaddy of all annoying travel questions: "Are we there yet?" That's a great question to ask—especially when your brother is bothering you and your Nintendo DS has run out of batteries and your bladder can no longer contain the small ocean of soda you slammed at the last pit stop. (Beware the sixty-four-ounce super slurper!)

In Daniel's vision, he sees a "holy one," who, after witnessing the overthrow of

Study Questions

Many people who study the prophecies about the little horn view the Catholic Church as the worst entity on earth. Do you think they make a valid point, given its religious framework? Do you see other entities as being more dangerous?

Notes

_____

_____

_____

_____

_____

_____

_____

_____

_____

_____

_____

_____

_____

_____

_____

_____

_____

_____

_____

_____

_____

_____

the sanctuary and the "continual" (our friend *tamid*) being taken away from the Prince of the host, asks another "holy one," "*For how long* is the vision concerning the continual [*tamid*] burnt offering, the transgression that makes desolate [a phrase that refers to the actions of both pagan and Christian Rome], and the giving over of the sanctuary and host to be trampled under foot?" (Daniel 8:13; emphasis added).

"How long?" means "Are we there yet?"

As bad as being crammed in a van for a multihour expedition with your family can be, it doesn't come close to seeing God's house be torn apart. That's excruciatingly painful, and the sooner it's over, the better. Thankfully, an answer comes—though it causes Daniel great distress. "And he said to him, 'For two thousand and three hundred evenings and mornings [days]; then the sanctuary shall be restored to its rightful state' " (verse 14).

Daniel writes that he "sought to understand" the vision. Thankfully, as in chapter 7, Gabriel shows up with some answers—but not all the answers Daniel would like to have. Gabriel tells Daniel that the vision "is for the time of the end" (verse 17; compare verse 19)—meaning that while Daniel has every right to be concerned, the prophecy won't be fulfilled until the distant future, when earth's history will be wrapping up. Then Gabriel tells Daniel, "seal up the vision, for it pertains to many days hence" (verse 26).

"Are we there yet, God?"

"Sorry, Dan, not even close, not until the end of time."

Naturally, Daniel "was overcome [by grief] and lay sick for some days" (verse 27). As when you're taking a test and you have to leave the space after a question blank, Daniel has to leave this prophetic riddle unanswered.

So, it's been thousands of years since Daniel's day. Do we know anything about this vision now? Are we there yet?

"Yes," and "Almost."

In the nineteenth century, William Miller and many other people all over the world looked at the way history was unfolding and began to study the prophecies of Daniel and Revelation intensely.[1] New information came to light not only through their intense study but also from their deep experiences with God.

Here's what they discovered. In the Old Testament, the sanctuary—and later the temple—was "cleansed" once a year in a special service known as the Day of Atonement. (Check out Leviticus 16 and chapter 24 of my book *What We Believe for Teens*.) On this special day, the high priest performed a special sacrifice in addition to the regular sacrifices that were offered every day throughout the year. And, as part of his ministry on that day, he entered the second compartment of the sanctuary, which was known as the Holy of Holies or the Most Holy Place.

Cleaning a filthy temple

Throughout the year, people offered thousands of sacrifices in the sanctuary, confessing their sins, which, through the ministry of the priests, were then symbolically transferred from the sinners to the sanctuary. After a year of sacrifices, the sanctuary tended to look a bit gory (and probably smelled special too). But more important, it was defiled by the guilt of all the sins that had been transferred there. So the sanctuary needed to be cleansed.

Two male goats were used in the service held on the Day of Atonement (Leviticus 16:5). The high priest sacrificed one, "the goat of the sin offering," and used its blood to cleanse the sanctuary "from the uncleannesses of the people of Israel" (verses 15, 19). Then he symbolically transferred the sins to the second goat, which bore them away to an uninhabited place—thus symbolizing the removal of sin from the universe. In Leviticus, God tells the result of that day—the point of that service: "on this day shall atonement be made for you, to cleanse you; from all your sins you shall be clean before the LORD" (verse 30).

As we have already seen, the Old Testament sanctuary points to the heavenly sanctuary. What's more, at the "time of the end," the Jewish temple no longer exists. (Remember Rome's fire-starting shenanigans?) So Daniel's prophecy about restoring the sanctuary (Daniel 8:14) must be pointing to the heavenly sanctuary and to our heavenly High Priest—Jesus.

The Bible says as much: "Thus it was necessary for the copies of the heavenly things to be purified with these rites, but the heavenly things themselves with better sacrifices than these. For Christ has entered, not into a sanctuary made with hands, a copy of the true one, but into heaven itself, now to appear in the presence of God on our behalf" (Hebrews 9:23, 24). So, after the Resurrection, Jesus ascended to heaven as our High Priest. However, if the Old Testament sanctuary is a copy of the heavenly one, then Jesus' taking on the role of High Priest means He would have a special cleansing ministry to perform resembling what the earthly high priests did on the symbolical days of atonement.

The prophecy, then, means that at the end of the 2,300 days (2,300 literal years), Jesus *begins* a final cleansing ministry in the heavenly sanctuary that will end when earth's history ends. This special phase of ministry, known as the "investigative judgment," is Jesus' final judgment before the Second Coming, when He returns to earth to carry out the "sentences" determined by that judgment.

Some people picture the judgment at the end of the world as involving all of earth's people standing in a long line (like the line at Space Mountain in Disneyland, for instance) in front of God, who is sitting on a throne and holding a large gavel and deciding the fate of every person who ever lived. However, when Jesus comes to earth again, it isn't to *make* judgments—it's to *deliver* them. When He comes, He will gather all His people. They'll "meet the Lord in the air; and so we shall always be with the Lord" (1 Thessalonians 4:17). So, in the special phase of ministry Jesus carries out in heaven, He's making His final judgments *before* coming to earth to carry them out. At that time God's character is revealed, and the wicked character of the little horn and all its followers becomes apparent.

Study Questions

Part of the fight that goes on during the 2,300 years concerns conflicts between tradition and the Bible. Why do people have such a hard time changing their views? What makes traditions so hard to give up even when you have evidence that they conflict with Scripture?

_____

_____

_____

_____

_____

_____

_____

_____

_____

_____

_____

_____

_____

_____

_____

_____

Notes

Daniel learned in the vision of chapter 8 that the special "investigative judgment" begins at the end of the 2,300 days (years). But to know when that period ends, we have to know when it begins. What date is the starting point for our calculations?

Daniel says he doesn't understand the vision. He didn't know what the starting point was, and neither do we . . . yet.

CHAPTER 14 IN BRIEF

While Jesus our High Priest is in heaven, we have to grapple with forces on earth that try to turn our attention away from Him and to distort the picture we have of Him. That can be as simple as feeling sleepy during prayer or having someone text you during church, or it can be as complicated as having a mean-spirited religious leader bully you toward accepting something that doesn't add up in Scripture. The spirit of the little horn is still alive and well, unfortunately. Where do you see it at work in your life? What distracts you from the loving Savior who "is able for all time to save those who draw near to God through him, since he always lives to make intercession for them" (Hebrews 7:25)?

Without Jesus' intercession for us, we have no hope of salvation. We can't make ourselves good enough to get into heaven, so we desperately need a High Priest there who will help us as we struggle through the challenges of this earth. By holding on to Him as our Advocate in heaven, we can be confident that God will save us regardless of life's little horns doing everything they can to distract us. Even if the unpleasant present seems to go on and on.

Having a history—whether yours consists of ten years or one hundred—means having traditions. Some traditions are good and have tremendous meaning—for instance, giving gifts at Christmas and setting off moderate explosions on Independence Day. However, sometimes well-intentioned people can see genuine needs and in their efforts to fulfill those needs, they may develop traditions that don't align with God's Word. As we interact with members of other faith traditions, it is important that we ask good questions that don't assume evil intentions. Be friendly and curious, and share your own faith discoveries in the hope that, ultimately, everyone will find truth and a clearer picture of God will emerge. Never force your faith on anyone—it's the little horn, and not God, who uses coercion.

And remember: though a little horn can be extremely powerful, his power will be broken (Daniel 8:25), and Jesus will restore this world to the paradise He created it to be.

ENDNOTE

1. See chapter 24 of my book *What We Believe for Teens* (Nampa, Idaho: Pacific Press®, 2007).

Chapter 15
Prayer of the Prophet
(Daniel 9)

Study Question

Daniel read the prophecies of Jeremiah. What does this imply for you and me about studying the Bible?

_____

_____

_____

_____

_____

_____

_____

_____

_____

_____

_____

_____

_____

_____

_____

_____

_____

_____

_____

_____

_____

"You see, I *am* a prophet of God."

I've a heard people make a lot of interesting statements during Bible studies, but someone's declaration that he holds prophetic office is among the most interesting —if not profoundly disturbing.

One of my church members had been studying with a friendly young man who had been attending our church. I stopped by to leave some extra study materials, and that's when this man—whom I'll call Jim—looked us both in the eye and gave us his testimony.

I thought briefly about saying, "Well, how interesting," and then turning to my church member and saying, "I must be going now—lots of things to do today that don't involve being here at this moment." But I decided to stay. After all, prophets have messages. Jim had things to share, and I wanted to hear them.

Jim said that God informed him of many things; among them, that he'd win three hundred million dollars in the lottery and would marry a supermodel. He kept track of these prophecies in spiral notebooks.

Naturally, I was suspicious when Jim said Jesus would in essence rig the lottery on behalf of His people and that He would select a woman to be Jim's companion, the criterion being her appearance. But I let Jim finish, and then we prayed together, ending the study—but not the prophetic problem.

Jim told me—another prophetic message—that he needed to meet with me and another leader of our church because, he said, if we couldn't accept him as a prophet, he couldn't continue attending our church.

Though I did believe then, and still do, that God was leading in Jim's life, I didn't believe him to be a prophet. However, I wanted to avoid outright rejection because Jim had been attending our church faithfully and contributing to its life.

Jim didn't have a mean personality or a critical spirit, and, as far as I could tell, he didn't want to preach to us. He just wanted to have his status acknowledged—a status about which I believe he was confused. God had been working strongly in his life, leading him to the truth. Unfortunately, instead of accepting that as meaning simply that he was a child of God whom the Spirit was leading, Jim had interpreted it to mean that God was making him a prophet. The "prophetic words" that Jim spoke revolved around his moving up the socioeconomic ladder. That made me wonder whether he simply needed some affirmation and support. In any case, we scheduled a meeting, and I began to pray.

I told God that while I knew Jim wasn't a prophet, he was a friend, and I didn't want to see him leave, but I couldn't violate my conscience or my knowledge of the Bible and declare him to be a prophet. "God," I said, "I don't know what to do, so You'd better do something. Please help!"

At our next meeting, we looked through several of Jim's spiral notebooks, noting the prophecies written in them. Then, suddenly, Jim put them away and announced that he was going to the heart of the matter—he was going to ask God to prove to us that he was a prophet. At that point, I began to pray too—but not for God to prove that Jim was a prophet. No, I was praying that He would reveal the truth.

Jim offered praise to the Lord and then made his request. He asked for direct proof that God had made him a prophet. He prayed, "Circle us with a ring of light."

I'm a fan of light, and I see no problems with it appearing in a ring formation. However, in this case I must say rings and lights didn't appeal to me. Instead, I had this panicky thought: *What if there* is *a ring of light when I open my eyes?*

But when Jim said his "Amen" and we all opened our eyes, we saw . . . nothing. Well, nothing but a desk and chairs and bookcases basking in the glow of the only source of light in the room—a lightbulb, and a dim one at that. Jim paused a moment and then quietly thanked us for our time and began preparing to leave.

We stopped him and offered him some encouragement; but he was embarrassed. He let us pray with him, and then he left, and I haven't seen him since. Being confronted with the hard reality of his prophetic status—or lack of it—had to have been a difficult experience. I hope his spiritual vision is clearer now, and I wish him well wherever he is.

I think many times the term *false prophet* raises images of men (and women) in dark robes, pointy black beards (well, probably not the women), and red eyes, doing their best to undermine God. I'm sure there have been false prophets who had nefarious intentions. But that's not always the case. Sometimes people who mean well want to help, and they offer a word in the name of the Lord without realizing the painful consequences that follow when that word really comes from their imagination.

Consequences of false prophecy

Jeremiah prophesied in Daniel's day, especially during the destruction of Jerusalem under the leadership of King Nebuchadnezzar. God gave Jeremiah the unpleasant task of telling His people not to fight but simply to let Babylon take them captive. People didn't respond well to Jeremiah's messages—one time throwing him into a giant pot full of mud (see Jeremiah 38).

In the midst of trying to communicate a message about as popular as a poke in the eye, Jeremiah had to deal with false prophets who were saying exactly the opposite of what God wanted people to hear, and they claimed to be speaking for the Lord. One such case was Hananiah, who claimed that God told him, "I have broken the yoke of the king of Babylon. Within two years I will bring back to this place all the vessels of the LORD's house, which Nebuchadnezzar king of Babylon took away from this place and carried to Babylon" (Jeremiah 28:2, 3).

Jeremiah's response?

Surprisingly supportive.

He said, "Amen! May the LORD do so; may the LORD make the words which you have prophesied come true, and bring back to this place from Babylon the vessels of the house of the LORD, and all the exiles" (verse 6).

Not surprisingly, however, Jeremiah had more to say, and his message was less than cheery. "Yet hear now this word which I speak in your hearing and in the hearing of all the people. The prophets who preceded you and me from ancient times prophesied war, famine, and pestilence against many countries and great kingdoms. As for the prophet who prophesies peace, when the word of that prophet comes to pass, then it will be known that the LORD has truly sent the prophet" (verses 7–9).

Alas, while Hananiah gave a positive message, what he said was not from the Lord. And because contradicting the word of the Lord—who was telling the Jews to surrender to Babylon—led to the death of those people who believed him, it cost Hananiah everything he had. Jeremiah had the final word (which *was* from the Lord): "Listen, Hananiah, the LORD has not sent you, and you have made this people trust in a lie. Therefore thus says the LORD: 'Behold, I will remove you from the face of the earth. This very year you shall die, because you have uttered rebellion against the LORD' " (verses 15, 16).

The word of a prophet should be taken seriously. Daniel 9 pictures Daniel doing that.

Riveting reading

Every so often a book comes along that compels you to read into the wee hours of the morning. Somehow the content grabs you so strongly that you can't sleep, eat, or speak to anyone because all your attention is focused on the pages you hold in your hand. I have no doubt you've experienced that feeling while reading this book, and while I am flattered, you really need to eat and get to bed. You could also use a shower.

Remember, you can read more tomorrow.

Thirteen years after Daniel saw a vision he couldn't understand, while he was reading a scroll that his older prophetic pal Jeremiah had written (see Daniel 8:27; 9:1, 2), Daniel came across Jeremiah 29:10, which says, "Thus says the LORD: When seventy years are completed for Babylon, I will visit you, and I will fulfill to you my promise and bring you back to this place." In other words, Daniel's people would be held captive in Babylon for seventy years, and then they would be released.

Study Question

See if you can reproduce the seventy-week/490-year timeline using only the accounts in Daniel 8 and 9.

Like a child sitting on the stairs and patiently counting down the minutes until his timeout ends, Daniel does the math and comes to a startling realization: Jerusalem was destroyed in 605 B.C., Babylon has fallen to the Medes and the Persians (just like the prophecy said), and now, in the year 538 B.C., Darius, son of Ahasuerus (no, that's not a dinosaur), sits on the throne (Daniel 9:1).

That means sixty-eight of the seventy years have passed.

Which means only two years are left.

Which means something big is about to happen. The riveting read in Daniel's hands is about to become a reality. The story will suck them all in.

So, Daniel determines to get some answers before the time is up.

What's the answer?

Remember taking a test in school and discovering you knew every single answer to every single question—except one? One minute you're filling in tiny circles at the speed of light, and the next minute all circle-shading stops as you stare blankly at the rogue question your teacher never warned you about—and that perfect score you're so close to achieving hangs in the balance as the clock sprints toward the deadline. You wrack your brain for any information that might help:

What you ate for breakfast.

The square root of 144.

News headlines.

The weather report.

But nothing helps. You're stuck.

For the first time in his career, Daniel doesn't have the light he needs to understand the vision he's seen. He could interpret King Nebuchadnezzar's dreams (chapters 2 and 4), the handwriting on the wall (chapter 5), and his own dream of the animal kingdoms (chapter 7). He has even been given insight into the little horn that shows up in chapters 7 and 8. But Daniel 8 ends with Daniel saying he "was overcome and lay sick for some days" because he "was appalled by the vision and did not understand it" (verse 27). The angel has explained everything in the vision except those 2,300 days. Daniel seems to be saying that wondering about them has made him ill. It's like a retired pastor being asked to speak last minute but not being able to remember any of the sermons he has preached.

Now, on the eve of his people's release, Daniel is at his wit's end, wanting to know what is going on. He needs an answer to a test on which he's been doing so well up to this point.

Someone must know.

Someone must be able to tell him.

It's time to pray.

Prayer of the prophet

Daniel's prayer runs from verse 3 to verse 19, and even then he stops only because help has come (Daniel 9:20, 21). This demonstrates that Daniel isn't just reciting some common before-bedtime prayer. His heart and mind are completely engaged in seeking God. The prayer is beautiful and worth a read. I'll point out just a couple of key ideas.

For starters, Daniel wasn't praying for just himself. At the very end of the prayer, he says, "O Lord, hear; O Lord, forgive; O Lord, give heed and act; delay not, for thy own sake, O my God, because thy city and thy people are called by thy name" (verse 19). Daniel has based the entire prayer on what God said He would do—namely, forgive and save His people.

Unlike the self-focused prayer of Hananiah ("don't anyone panic; captivity will last only two years") or even Jim ("God's going to give me money and women"), Daniel keeps God at the center of his concern. That's a good reminder for us. Too often our prayers are really about us:

"God, I'm broke. Give me some money."
"God, I'm sick. Make me feel better."
"God, I'm bored. Show up and entertain me."
"God, I'm hungry. Make me a sandwich."

While God loves to bless us, waiting on us hand and foot isn't His sole purpose for being. In fact, on the contrary—we're to wait on and serve Him.

Second, a large portion of Daniel's prayer involves confessing sins and shortcomings: "We have sinned and done wrong and acted wickedly and rebelled, turning aside from your commandments and rules. We have not listened to your servants the prophets, who spoke in your name to our kings, our princes, and our fathers, and to all the people of the land" (verses 5, 6). It seems weird, but it's true: Daniel uses the word *we* when he confesses Judah's sins of disobeying God and ignoring His prophets. Daniel himself is a prophet, so what on earth is he doing? It's one thing to pray for other people who are disobedient—but to include yourself? Maybe he's praying too fervently and his mind is overloaded.

Or maybe he's a *true* prophet, so he understand that no one is as good as God and that everyone needs His help—even prophets. As a *true* prophet, he also has a love for God's people, *his* people, and he includes himself in his prayer because he considers their fate to be his—like your family, as goofy as they are, is still your family, and your connection to them is permanent.

Prophets are bold, but not arrogant; angry, but not unloving; powerful, but not perfect. Therefore Daniel prays intensely for himself and his people.

Gabriel gives answers

Sometimes when I was taking a test in school and was stuck on a question no one else seemed to understand either, a miracle happened. The teacher would interrupt our anguish and point out a flaw with the question or acknowledge that no one has been able to answer it—so the teacher drops it from the test and just gives the answer to the

Study Question

Read Numbers 12:6; 24:4, 16; Deuteronomy 18:21, 22; Isaiah 8:19, 20; Jeremiah 28:9; Daniel 10:17, 18; Matthew 7:15, 16; 1 Corinthians 14:3; 2 Peter 1:20, 21; and 1 John 4:1–3, and then make a list of at least ten "tests" that determine whether or not a prophet is true.

class. Something like that happened for Daniel. As he was wrestling with God in prayer, an answer interrupted him in the form of the angel Gabriel. The angel says, "O Daniel, I have now come out to give you insight and understanding. At the beginning of your pleas for mercy a word went out, and I have come to tell it to you, for you are greatly loved. Therefore consider the word and understand the vision" (verses 22, 23).

As soon as Daniel began to pray, God sent an answer. God has no voicemail; He hears our prayers immediately. Gabriel affirmed God's love for Daniel and His desire that Daniel understand "the vision." At long last, the vision that had perplexed Daniel ever since he saw the ram and the goat and heard the two holy ones talking will begin to come together.

The answer comes encrypted in a timeline of prophetic weeks. Using our "day for a year" principle, we can unlock and unveil the most important prophecy in the book of Daniel. It's a prophecy that reaches way beyond the release of the Jews and their return to their homeland. This prophecy pinpoints the coming of the "anointed one"—otherwise known as the Messiah.

Seventy weeks

Gabriel says, "Seventy weeks of years are decreed about your people" (verse 24). The Hebrew word translated "decreed" has the nuance of something being *cut off* from a larger whole. It's like slicing a piece of pie for yourself before serving it to your company.

The angel says the seventy weeks are cut off from a larger period to give time for, among other things, the anointing of "a most holy place" (verse 24). The idea here— which we explored in the previous chapter—is to allow time for the transition from the earthly sanctuary to the heavenly sanctuary, where Jesus serves as the High Priest.

The angel goes on to say that "from the going forth of the command to restore and build Jerusalem until Messiah the Prince, there shall be seven weeks and sixty-two weeks" (verse 25, NKJV). Some translations try to separate the seven weeks and the sixty-two weeks into two different time periods, but in the original language they go together to make sixty-nine weeks. So, sixty-nine prophetic weeks would pass from whenever the command was given to rebuild broken Jerusalem until the "anointed one" was to appear.

Date of the command

The prophecy tells us how much time would pass till the Messiah would come, and it tells us what the starting point is—"the going forth of the word to restore and build Jerusalem" (verse 25). To know when to expect the Messiah to come, all a person had to do was to find the date of that "word," that decree.

The book of Ezra (another prophet) tells us there were three different decrees made by human beings that had to do with the rebuilding of Jerusalem: "And the elders of the Jews built and prospered through the prophesying of Haggai the prophet and Zechariah the son of Iddo. They finished their building by decree of the God of Israel and by decree of Cyrus and Darius and Artaxerxes king of Persia" (Ezra 6:14).

So, which decree do we take as the starting point of the seventy-week prophecy?

Cyrus (mercifully, unrelated to Miley) issued the first decree in 538 B.C.—but his decree involved only the temple and the first wave of exiles to return. Darius made his decree in 519 B.C., but it just confirmed the one Cyrus had made. The decree that Artaxerxes made in 457 B.C. was the one that got the job done—finishing the work on the temple and especially, restoring political power to the Jews.

The "word" was given in 457 B.C.

The formula

So there's another formula.

Start time: 457 B.C.

Sixty-nine prophetic weeks = 483 prophetic days.

Four hundred eighty-three prophetic days = 483 literal years.

So, if we start at 457 B.C. and time-travel 483 years into the future, we arrive at A.D. 27.

How easy was that? I should have taught math . . . or time travel.

But now that we have arrived in A.D. 27, what are we looking for? The prophecy says, "the coming of an anointed one" (Daniel 7:25). Flipping forward a few books from Daniel, we arrive at the Gospels, which record an important event that occurred at this time—the baptism of Jesus.

The Gospel of Luke says, "In the fifteenth year of the reign of Tiberius Caesar" "Jesus also had been baptized and was praying, the heavens were opened, and the Holy Spirit descended on him in bodily form, like a dove; and a voice came from heaven, 'You are my beloved Son; with you I am well pleased' " (Luke 3:1, 21, 22).

What was Tiberius's fifteenth year as emperor?

A.D. 27.

Interestingly enough, John the Baptist doesn't feel worthy to baptize Jesus, but Jesus tells him, "Let it be so now, for thus it is fitting for us to *fulfill* all righteousness" (Matthew 3:15; emphasis added). Echoing this phrase, Mark records Jesus as saying, "The *time is fulfilled,* and the kingdom of God is at hand; repent and believe in the gospel" (Mark 1:15; emphasis added).

Jesus was baptized at the end of the "sixty-nine weeks."

Hastily Drawn Figure 15.1

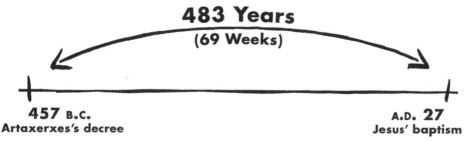

483 Years
(69 Weeks)

457 B.C.
Artaxerxes's decree

A.D. 27
Jesus' baptism

Study Question

How do we know that Daniel 9 is related to the 2,300 days of Daniel 8?

One week left to complete the "seventy weeks."
This week is brutal.

Cut off

The film *127 Hours* tells the true story of hiker Aron Ralston—in all of its gory details. When Aron was hiking in a slot canyon in Utah's Canyonlands National Park, he slipped as he was negotiating some large rocks in the canyon. Everyone takes a tumble from time to time; but rarely do we have a boulder follow us and then wedge itself in the narrow canyon, pinning our right hand between itself and the canyon wall. You can imagine Aron's joy when he couldn't free his appendage. His joy was further enhanced by the hard reality facing him: he could stay stuck and die in the wilderness, or he could *cut off his hand* and find freedom.

Aron chose life, but at what a cost! After a failed attempt to saw through the flesh and bone of his forearm with a dull pocket knife, he deliberately breaks the bones in his forearm and then finishes the job with the dull pocket knife. Then, leaving his severed hand behind, he hurries out of that canyon so he can get help before he bleeds to death.

Excuse me while I shudder.

As horrifying as the tale is, I have tremendous admiration for Aron's will to live. He is now married and has a son . . . and he's doing well financially from his book and movie deals. Maybe I should find a way to cut my arm off . . .

What does this have to do with our prophecy? Well, Scripture says, "After the sixty-two weeks, an *anointed one shall be cut off* and shall have nothing. . . . And he shall *make a strong covenant* with many for one week, *and for half of the week* he shall put an end to sacrifice and offering" (verses 26, 27; emphasis added).

The "anointed one" is the Messiah, and the Messiah is "cut off" in the process of making a "strong covenant" or "agreement" with many.

How can cutting someone off be of any benefit?

We hate being cut off when we're talking.

We hate being cut off in traffic.

We hate being cut off from the precious electricity that runs our house.

Unless it was a matter of life and death—as it was for Aron Ralston—I don't see any benefit of cutting anything off. But that's just what this prophecy is about: life and death—spiritual and physical.

We can infer from the text that while the Messiah—Jesus—makes a "strong covenant" for one week, when that week comes to the halfway point, He is "cut off" and "puts an end to sacrifice and offering."

So what happened?

The seventieth week

One prophetic week = seven prophetic days.

Seven prophetic days = seven literal years.

Time-travel seven years from Jesus' baptism in A.D. 27, and you arrive at A.D. 34.

The halfway point between the spring of A.D. 27 and the spring of A.D. 34 is the fall of A.D. 31.

What happened to Jesus in the fall of that year? How was He cut off?

"Pilate said to them, 'Then what shall I do with Jesus who is called Christ?' They all said, 'Let him be *crucified*!' " (Matthew 27:22; emphasis added).

Jesus was executed for our sins in A.D. 31. He was cut off from life for three days. Scholars calculate the year based on the fact that the Gospels record four Passovers that Jesus celebrated between His baptism in A.D. 27 and His death.

As for "putting an end to sacrifice and offering," Scripture says that after His death, "the curtain of the temple was torn in two, from top to bottom" (Mark 15:38).

What does that have to do with sacrifices and offerings? The curtain was made of heavy, thick fabric. It separated people from the Most Holy Place, where the presence of God dwelt. Jesus' death to save us from sin fixed our broken relationship with God. The tearing of the temple curtain symbolized that we no longer need human priests and rituals of worship in order to access God—we can reach Him ourselves through Jesus Christ.

When Jesus rose from the dead (freaking out a bunch of Roman soldiers and causing them to pass out), He told His disciples, "Thus it is written, that the Christ should suffer and on the third day rise from the dead, and that repentance and forgiveness of sins should be proclaimed in his name to all nations, beginning from Jerusalem" (Luke 24:46, 47). The good news of forgiveness and of a restored connection with God wasn't only for the Jews, but now was also meant for people of all nationalities. And it's this idea of the message of Jesus beginning to spread everywhere that dominates the remaining three and a half years of the final prophetic week, taking us to A.D. 34.

A major event happened in A.D. 34 that can be viewed both positively and negatively. The event is the tragic death of Stephen, who told off some stubborn Jewish leaders who didn't like what he said about Jesus (see Acts 7). Today, when we hear a sermon we don't like, we might dose through it or write a letter to the preacher telling him to do better next time or maybe even switch to another church. Back then, if people felt that someone's sermon was particularly offensive, they stoned the preacher. Stephen, unfortunately, didn't get a letter. He died under a pile of stones, becoming the first martyr (someone who dies for their faith) for Jesus. Many people have focused on this event as the failure for Israel and what has led to what is known as anti-Semitism (anti-Jewish words, thoughts, and behaviors).

But the second perspective is much better.

Up to that time, most of the believers had been living in Jerusalem and its suburbs; so for the most part, the good news about Jesus had been restricted to that

Study Question

How should we spend our time while we wait for God to answer our prayers?

_____

_____

_____

_____

_____

_____

_____

_____

_____

_____

_____

_____

_____

_____

_____

_____

_____

_____

_____

_____

_____

_____

_____

_____

_____

_____

_____

_____

_____

area. But after Stephen died, "there arose . . . a great persecution against the church in Jerusalem, and they were all scattered throughout the regions of Judea and Samaria. . . . Now those who were scattered went about preaching the word" (Acts 8:1, 4, ESV).

Just before Jesus ascended to heaven, He told His disciples, "You will be my witnesses in Jerusalem and in all Judea and Samaria, and to the end of the earth" (Acts 1:8, ESV). Now that progression had begun: at the end of the seventy weeks, the believers took the first steps toward sharing the good news about Jesus worldwide.

Hastily Drawn Figure 15.2

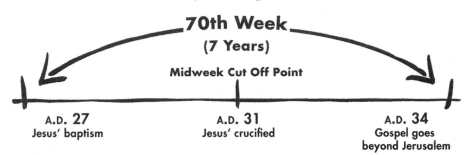

70th Week
(7 Years)

Midweek Cut Off Point

A.D. **27**
Jesus' baptism

A.D. **31**
Jesus' crucified

A.D. **34**
Gospel goes
beyond Jerusalem

The Prince who destroys

In Daniel 9:26, there's a negative little side note about a prince "who is to come" who will "destroy the city and sanctuary." Many scholars—Jewish and Christian—recognize this individual as Titus, who, with Roman firepower, leveled the city of Jerusalem and the temple in A.D. 70. The wording Jesus used in Matthew 24 to speak of this destruction parallels the wording in Daniel 9:26, 27.

Twenty-three hundred days and 1844

Gabriel's answer to the prayer of Daniel recorded in chapter 9 of his book gives us the starting date not only for the seventy-week prophecy but also for the time prophecy in the vision of chapter 8, the one that Daniel couldn't understand. The seventy weeks (490 years) and the 2,300 days (years) are part of the *same* timeline, which starts in 457 B.C. So, if the seventy weeks (490 years) that are "decreed" for Daniel's people ends in A.D. 34, then all we need to do is

subtract 490 from 2,300 = 1810 years left,
and time-travel 1,810 years into the future from A.D. 34—which brings us to 1844.

Jesus began the special second part of His ministry in the heavenly sanctuary in 1844.

According to Bible prophecy, then, we are living at the very end of earth's history. We've already reached and passed the end of the longest prophecy in the book of Daniel. That prophecy is fulfilled, and the only remaining event is for Jesus to come back and make this world new.

Hastily Drawn Figure 15.3

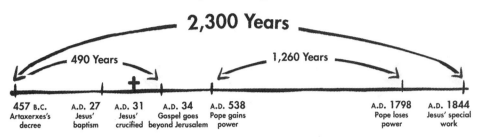

Did Daniel know all this?

No, he died long before Jesus lived on earth—to say nothing of the end of the 2,300 years. But Daniel did receive assurance from Gabriel that the Jews would be released from exile and that the Messiah would come.

CHAPTER 15 IN BRIEF

Daniel 9 demonstrates that God repeatedly breaks into human history and experience to accomplish His plans. We see that the prayers of God's people—when made in a humble spirit with the aim to glorify God—are answered *immediately.* This doesn't mean we will know or see everything God has in mind for His people; Daniel got the answers he needed for peace of mind, but didn't live to see everything accomplished. God gives us what we need.

This chapter also shows us that God doesn't play hide-and-seek with us. Daniel was disturbed that he didn't understand what God was doing, so God sent Gabriel with the express commission to "make him understand." God doesn't want to be confusing, even though life can be complex. He wants to be the One you can talk to and bring all your troubles and misunderstandings to. While God hears us instantly, it may take a while before understanding dawns in our minds. But know that God will reveal what we need as we seek Him earnestly, patiently, and honestly in prayer.

Chapter 16
VIP and the Beginning of the Last Vision
(Daniel 10)

I've been a Minnesota Vikings fan ever since my life began. This tragic American football team is the source of unspeakable disappointment for its fans, who keep cheering for the team year after agonizing year.

During the 2009 playoffs, my wayward Vikings actually stood a chance to be Super Bowl champions. The only obstacle was the game against the New Orleans Saints. By all accounts they had more than a great chance at defeating this team and giving Minnesota fans their long-awaited championship. What happened, however, was one of the greatest debacles in football history—at least for me and thousands of grieving Minnesotans.

I won't recount the entire exasperating experience (especially since I viewed the game with several vocal Saints fans, who piled insult on top of my emotional injuries . . . and the Vikings' physical ones). The most ire-inspiring moment for me was when our Hall of Fame quarterback Brett Favre tried to hand the ball to Adrian Peterson, one of the greatest running backs in the league.

By every reasonable expectation on planet Earth, these two superstar players should have been able to HAND the ball to each other. How many THOUSANDS of times had they done this in practice and in games? And they were only ONE STINKING YARD from the end zone (where you make touchdowns, score points, and do a dance). All year long Adrian Peterson had been hanging on to the football while five or more players from the opposing team hung on to him, trying to stop him from running. Time and again he carried the ball AND the opposing players to the end zone.

At this critical juncture in the most important game of the season, Brett and Adrian had a chance to score a touchdown that would have put the Vikings ahead.

All they had to do was to complete the handoff. No problem. Just as easy as passing the salt, handing in homework (provided you did it), or flushing the toilet—which is exactly where the game went when the ball was put into play.

Brett handed the ball to Adrian "Butterfingers" Peterson—and he dropped it.

Dropped it one yard from scoring a touchdown.

I almost grabbed my television and spiked it like a football after a touchdown.

And the horror didn't stop there. Before the atrocities were brought to an end in overtime, the Vikings had racked up six fumbles (which means they dropped the ball when everything that is good and decent in the world says they should have been able to hold on to it) and two interceptions (which is when your team's quarterback throws the ball to SOMEONE ON THE OTHER TEAM).

So, the Vikings lost (which means they sent their fans into sadness and shock). That was three years prior to the writing of this chapter, and let's just say the Vikings have shown no evidence that they will get near another playoff game before my children are grandparents.

What had been so promising is now a devastating memory, with little hope of reprieve for who knows how long.

A delay for Daniel's people

It's been two years since Daniel was visited by the angel (see the previous chapter), and prophecies given long before were rapidly being fulfilled. The exile of Daniel's people has ended after seventy years, just as Daniel had read in the book of Jeremiah. In addition, a royal decree has been issued for the rebuilding of Jerusalem—just as the angel Gabriel said would happen. You would expect Daniel to be as excited as a football fan watching his team win the Super Bowl, so it's a little strange that chapter 10 opens up with Daniel feeling a little depressed. "In those days I, Daniel, was mourning for three weeks. I ate no delicacies, no meat or wine entered my mouth, nor did I anoint myself at all, for the full three weeks" (Daniel 10:2, 3).

Daniel acts as though someone is dead (he's mourning, after all) and refuses to eat any of his favorite food. Knowing that most people celebrate great victories with copious amounts of foods smothered in cheese and/or chocolate and sugary sodas, it's a safe bet to assume that something has gone wrong with the return of the exiles.

As we saw in the previous chapter, history records *three* separate decrees given to facilitate the rebuilding of the temple. When people repeat commands, it's because they aren't being carried out—and instead of making progress toward fulfilling the decreed rebuilding of the temple, Daniel's team is being flagged for a "delay of game." The people living in and around Judah aren't happy to see the Jews return to their ancestral homeland. "Then the people of the land discouraged the people of Judah and made them afraid to build, and hired counselors against them to frustrate their purpose, all the days of Cyrus king of Persia" (Ezra 4:4, 5).

Notes

How does Daniel 10 relate to Daniel 11 and 12?

_____

_____

_____

_____

_____

_____

_____

_____

_____

_____

_____

_____

_____

_____

_____

_____

_____

_____

_____

_____

_____

_____

_____

While Daniel believes that the prophecy will win out and his people will restore their lands (in the same way that I hang on to the hope that the Vikings will win at least one game in the near future), that doesn't make waiting and watching as their plans are frustrated any less painful. So Daniel fasts and prays for three weeks, hoping for some answers.

Someone hears him.

Someone shows up.

Someone.

Extremely.

Powerful.

Vision of a VIP

The label VIP (very important person) can be used of government officials, famous musicians, movie stars, or simply people with a lot of money who are expected to attend an event and who either receive special accommodations (a huge hotel room with unlimited M&Ms in their favorite colors) or are expected to make a big impact on those attending. Case in point—_Sesame Street Live,_ featuring a certain fuzzy red monster.

MoMo is the name my eldest daughter, Maddie, gave to Elmo when she was two. Of all her assorted stuffed toys (bears, bunnies, and bugs), Elmo was the one that captured the love in her heart. We had Elmo movies that we had to ration carefully to our obsessive little girl, who repeatedly asked for more MoMo. So when our generous neighbors gave us all a birthday present of tickets to _Sesame Street Live,_ we knew that attending that show would be the experience of a lifetime.

We took our seats in the arena with thousands of children, ages two through five, who were eagerly anticipating the start of the show. When the room lights went out, and the stage lights came on, and the happiest music known to humankind began, and all kinds of colorful characters danced across the stage, the children (including Maddie) responded with pure awe.

Then _he_ walked out and greeted the crowd—the fuzzy, red, life-sized Elmo waved hello and asked how everyone was doing.

He was met with shocked silence.

He asked again.

More shock.

Elmo then began the evening's semieducational program about letters and numbers. When it was all over, my daughter still stood in shock—along with the other kids. She had seen Elmo, and the experience was overpowering.

But as overpowering as seeing Elmo was to my two-year-old, her experience wouldn't hold a candle to the impact of a certain being whom Daniel saw on the bank of the Tigris River. "I lifted up my eyes and looked, and behold, a man clothed in linen, whose loins were girded with gold of Uphaz. His body was like beryl, his face like the appearance of lightning, his eyes like flaming torches, his arms and legs like the gleam of burnished bronze, and the sound of his words like the noise of a multitude" (Daniel 10:5, 6).

This person arouses more shock in Daniel than Elmo did in the toddlers at *Sesame Street Live*. Daniel is in a group of people, but he alone sees the vision. Everyone else just trembles and runs away, leaving Daniel alone with him. Nothing says friendship like running away from a threat and leaving your friend behind! Of course, they couldn't help themselves—not when the alternative was facing *this* VIP. Even Daniel, who has seen a number of visions, has "no strength ... left" and essentially passes out with his face in the dirt (verses 7–9).

So who *is* this guy?

Identifying the VIP, Part 1

You can tell a lot about a person by the clothes they wear. People who wear jerseys enjoy sports (note that I said *enjoy*, not *play*). People who wear badges or medals are officers of some king (or they're mall security). And people who wear pajama pants in public usually shop at Wal-Mart.

The man in the vision has two key pieces of attire: linen clothing and a gold belt. Priests wore linen garments (Leviticus 6:10), and Daniel describes the gold as "pure" (*upaz* in Hebrew), which suggests this person is royalty.

Daniel also records this being's physical appearance—which is even more revealing. His body is like beryl, or chrysolite (Daniel 10:6), which is one of the stones on the breastplate of the high priest (Exodus 28:20). His face is like lightning (shocking), his skin like fiery bronze (now that's a good tan), and "the sound of his words like the noise of a multitude."

Another prophet had an encounter like Daniel's. In chapter 1 of his book, Ezekiel gives pretty much the same description of the "likeness" from heaven that he saw, and he calls it "the appearance of the likeness of the glory of the Lord" (Ezekiel 1:28). Like Daniel, Ezekiel falls on his face.

Furthermore, John the revelator describes a being he says is "like a son of man [compare Daniel 7:13], clothed with a long robe and with a golden girdle round his breast; . . . his eyes were like a flame of fire, his feet were like burnished bronze, refined in a furnace, and his voice was like the sound of many waters" (Revelation 1:13–15). And like both prophets before him, John falls face down on the ground.

When we compare the descriptions of this being given by the three prophets, and when we take note of their reactions, it's safe to say we aren't dealing with a common angel. Not even Gabriel draws such a strong reaction from Daniel.

Speaking of Gabriel: he arrives on the scene again to help Daniel process what's going on—and he explains not only the delay of the decree but also who this VIP is.

How would you define *spiritual warfare*? (Read Ephesians 6:12.)

_____

_____

_____

_____

_____

_____

_____

_____

_____

_____

_____

_____

_____

_____

_____

_____

_____

_____

_____

_____

_____

Another angelic answer

Daniel writes, "And behold, a hand touched me and set me trembling on my hands and knees. And he [the messenger from heaven] said to me, 'O Daniel, man greatly beloved, give heed to the words that I speak to you, and stand upright, for now I have been sent to you.' While he was speaking this word to me, I stood up trembling" (Daniel 10:10, 11). This angel says the same thing that chapter 9 tells us Gabriel said, so it's safe to assume that this angel is Gabriel.

But what took him so long? I mean, Daniel's been fasting and praying for nearly a month.

Gabriel starts out by telling Daniel that as soon as he began to pray, Gabriel was sent to help (verse 12). But, he says, "The prince of the kingdom of Persia withstood me [Gabriel] twenty-one days" (verse 13). Then, Gabriel says, Michael, one of the chief princes, came to help. Gabriel left him to deal with the Persian prince while he came to help Daniel understand what was to happen to his people "in the latter days" (verse 14).

In the first verse of this chapter, before Daniel tells us about his discouragement, he writes, "the word [some translations say "vision" or "revelation"] was true, and it was a great conflict. And he [Daniel] understood the word and had understanding of the vision" (verse 1). This is an important piece of the prophetic puzzle that is easily lost. The vision that Daniel witnesses—and that we are about to discuss—is of a "great conflict" or "great war." It's introduced in chapter 10 and continues through chapter 11 and on into chapter 12.

Just as in a substantive book the prologue sets the stage for all that follows, so Daniel 10 sets the stage for the final two chapters of the book of Daniel. The prophet lets us know from the very beginning that chapters 10 through 12 of his book are all connected and have to do with a great war—which is the reason Gabriel was delayed.

Spiritual warfare

Gabriel tells Daniel, "The prince of the kingdom of Persia withstood me twenty-one days" (verse 13). The prince of Persia spoken of here (not related to the video game *Prince of Persia*) could be King Cyrus's son Cambyses (a good name for a candy bar), who was a devout Zoroastrian (no affiliation with Zorro).

Zoroastrianism's god is named Ahura Mazda (not the car manufacturer). Zoroastrians believe him to be the creator and that all worship is due him. Naturally, there's a conflict between worship of Ahura Mazda and worship of Daniel's God.

But Gabriel's explanation raises a question: how could a mortal man withstand the power of an angel?

Scholars believe that there's a reference here to a force behind the human ruler of Persia. The Bible tells us that God and Satan are in a constant battle for humanity's allegiance—like a great football game, one that, instead of being played with footballs, is being played with the hearts of men and women everywhere (not literally, but metaphorically). When Adam and Eve disobeyed God way back in Genesis, all humankind fell into the hands of the devil. So God came up with a play in which He would strip the "ball" from Satan, causing him to fumble so God could recover us and take us home.

God has given you and me the power to choose which side we want to be on. So, while God is battling Satan on our behalf, you and I also have something to do. Cambyses aligned himself with the force opposed to God, so the powers opposed to God rallied around him to prevent God's people from rebuilding their home.

Puppets—like Elmo—provide us with another way to think of this relationship between humans and spiritual powers such as angels and demons. On one level we see Elmo dancing and singing—but out of our sight there are puppet masters who control all the movements. The prince of Persia allowed a dark spiritual force to pull his strings. In contrast, Daniel chose to work with the forces of light.

Gabriel says the Persian prince resisted him for twenty-one days, the exact amount of time Daniel spent in prayer. It's as if Daniel and Gabriel are fighting alongside each other—and then reinforcements come as a result of Daniel's continual communion with God. Human armies have special forces such as the Navy Seals or the Green Berets (or Chuck Norris). God's army is no different. Heaven's ultimate Warrior shows up and breaks the Persian puppet. "Michael, one of the chief princes, came to help me, so I left him there with the prince of the kingdom of Persia, and came to make you understand what is to befall your people in the latter days. For the vision is for days yet to come. . . . But I will tell you what is inscribed in the book of truth: there is none who contends by my side against these except Michael, your prince" (verses 13, 14, 21).

So, who is this Michael?

Identifying the VIP, Part 2

Who is this Michael? Well, the verse we've just read tells us He is a "prince." We also know He is in charge of Daniel's people (Daniel 12:1), and the book of Revelation says He is a great archangel who fought in the war in heaven before human history began, and He cast the devil and his demons out of heaven (Revelation 12:7, 8).

Scholars identify Michael with the impressive and terrifyingly awesome figure wearing the linen and the golden belt—the being who caused Daniel (and Ezekiel and John) to pass out. But this still doesn't really give us a complete explanation of who this epically powerful prince is. We need a quick review to fully establish the identity of this divine figure.

- His name, *Michael,* means "who is like God."
- His clothes befit a king and a high priest.

- His physical description matches that of Jesus Christ in Revelation 1:13–15.
- And the facts that He has the authority to throw Satan out of heaven and that He rules over God's people tell us He is none other than Jesus Christ.

WARNING: Many people think that identifying Jesus with Michael the Archangel means that we think Jesus is a created being and that He's not God. That's an erroneous conclusion. We believe that Jesus is eternal and divine. Archangel is a title, not a description of His nature.

CHAPTER 16 IN BRIEF

Daniel 10 is about spiritual warfare—about human beings participating in the great battle that God and Satan are fighting for their hearts. Daniel is discouraged by the delays his people face; but after he prays, he has a vision in which Gabriel provides some answers. In that vision Daniel also sees Michael —Jesus Christ—to be a powerful divine Being who battles the powers of darkness and works on behalf of Daniel's people. The whole chapter sets up the remainder of the vision, which concerns various conflicts described in Daniel 11 and 12.

Every day you and I are faced with the same experience Daniel had. We are confronted by situations that discourage us and shake our faith, and we have to choose how we will respond. We can wallow in despair and depres-sion, or, like Daniel, we can pray despite our disappointments. Sometimes the answers won't come right away, but that's because there's a spiritual war—a "great war," as Daniel puts it—being fought around us. So, we must have patience and trust.

The good news is that even when there is a delay due to the battles being fought by angels and demons, God still hears our prayers as soon as we pray, and He goes right to work on our behalf. And the good news is that our Lord Jesus Christ (Prince Michael) is a warrior of heroic proportions whom no one can withstand—and He is on our side. We all have our own princes of Persia who work to frustrate our plans. But if we hold on, we'll see breakthroughs. Daniel was well loved in heaven, but even he had to wait for an answer.

Prayer is a weapon we can use when we feel powerless. Through prayer we can fight alongside our God and His angels. God doesn't need our help, but He chooses to include us. Take time not only to pray about the battles you face every day but about the battles others fight as well.

Chapter 17
Puzzles
(Daniel 11)

The picture on the box inspires me to try.

The reality of the thousand little pieces of cardboard cut in odd shapes tempts me to quit and maybe to burn the box and all those infernal pieces.

Every time I have made the decision to sit down and put a large jigsaw puzzle together, my will to see the project through to completion is severely tested. Finding the four corners is a breeze. Locating the corresponding edge pieces is a delightful challenge. It's those countless middle pieces that bring on the wild puzzle-burning frenzies and the trips to the psych ward. So many of them look like they're made for each other but don't fit together when I try them, which create these feelings of frustration.

Until I look at the picture again.

That big picture on the box helps orient me to what I'm seeing on each of the little pieces. Then the mess of colored cardboard pieces becomes meaningful, and suddenly I can start assembling them. Whenever I've succeeded at putting a jigsaw puzzle together, I've had the box in full view. It keeps me informed and focused.

As we move into the middle part of the final vision given to Daniel, we absolutely must keep the big picture in front of us at all times because this prophecy has a lot of tiny pieces, and we're still not sure where many of them go.

Daniel 11 is long and incredibly detailed and its language differs somewhat from that of the other vision chapters. There are no beasts or horns or other obvious symbols. Instead, there are kings and places and political intrigue—meaning plots and plans (not to be confused with pots and pans, although they're important too). This part of the vision pictures numerous conflicts, and if we don't keep our wits about us, the details will sidetrack us, and we'll lose the big picture.

Arriving at an understanding of Daniel 11's prophecy can be as difficult as putting a large jigsaw puzzle together upside down. As we go through this chapter, I'll do my best to turn each piece over; however, I won't go into as much detail as some

Notes

other books about Daniel do. (For more detail, see the suggested reading list at the back of this book.) We'll look at the big picture, briefly consider some of the pieces that have been turned over, and try a couple of ways of putting them together. With that in mind, it's time to explore the most difficult chapter in the book of Daniel.

The big picture

When I was growing up, my parents always conducted a curious ritual before we embarked on our annual vacation. They informed us that as a precaution against becoming sick on the trip, we needed to take some medicine. The elixir of choice was Benadryl—a concoction known not only for its healing properties but also for its remarkable ability to cause sleepiness. As we deduced later, the reason for this treatment wasn't so much to prevent illness as to prevent the bickering, fighting, and hyperactivity my siblings and I specialized in. Four wild kids in a van for four hours induced formidable feelings of frustration in our parents.

And we kids had in our repertoire many methods for inducing brawls. For instance, we used lame insults on each other. My sister's name is Kristal. Her loving brothers, including me, broke her name apart and turned it into Kris's Stall. There's a good chance that's the dumbest insult ever conceived—but it worked at getting a reaction out of her—which then inspired an angry response from our parents, telling us all to be quiet.

But our favorite way of passing the time was a dumb game called Touched You Last. The goal of the game was to touch the sibling next to us . . . well . . . last. We'd poke someone in the arm and say "Touched you last," and that brother or sister would respond in like manner. The problem was that the touching grew increasingly aggressive as each of us tried to end the game with the force of his or her "touch." This meant that "touched you last" became "shoved you last," which morphed into "punched you last" and finally ended with "drop-kicked you in the face last." The game usually ended with one of us in tears and with our parents threatening to turn the van around and end the vacation.

With all our insulting and fighting and carrying on, we frequently made the van rock from side to side. At that, my father would yell something, such as "Why is the van moving?" At least once, we made the mistake of responding, "Because you're driving it."

So, our poor parents tried drugging us before the trip, and they pinched us, threatened us, and even made one of us lie on the van floor between the shotgun seat and the driver's seat in a desperate attempt to separate us—to prevent conflict.

Daniel 11 is all about conflict.

Lots of it.

Daniel 10 introduced the theme of spiritual warfare. In Daniel 11 and 12, we see that theme played out till the end of time. The great battles described here—both earthly and spiritual—started in the time of the Medes and Persians and fit with the timelines of Daniel 2, 7, and 8.

Nearly all Bible scholars agree on the meaning of the first four verses of Daniel

Study Question

How can we study prophecy without getting lost in the details of chapters like this one?

11. The angel who is conveying the interpretation to Daniel says, "And now I will show you the truth. Behold, three more kings shall arise in Persia; and a fourth shall be far richer than all of them; and when he has become strong through his riches, he shall stir up all against the kingdom of Greece" (Daniel 11:2).

Then the angel reminds Daniel, who is living under Persian rule, of what he has known since he was told what Nebuchadnezzar's dream of the statue and his own vision of the animal kingdoms meant: Greece comes next.

The angel put it this way: "A mighty king shall arise, who shall rule with great dominion and do according to his will. And when he has arisen, his kingdom shall be broken and divided toward the four winds of heaven, but not to his posterity, nor according to the dominion with which he ruled; for his kingdom shall be plucked up and go to others besides these" (verses 3, 4).

This "mighty king" is, of course, Alexander the Great. We know that he dropped dead when he was in his early thirties, and that four of his generals divided his kingdom among themselves (another possible application of the "four winds of heaven"). In all this, the angel's message fits with historicism. (Remember, historicists believe that Daniel's prophecies extend from the time of Daniel himself to the time of the end.)

So far, this stuff is as easy as saying your own name. You might be tempted to think that the rest will be simple too. We already know that Rome follows Greece; that Rome becomes "Christian"; that the little horn emerges from Rome and persecutes God's people; that true Christianity and false Christianity have an epic clash that doesn't end until Jesus comes; and that then, He takes all true Christians to heaven until God redoes the earth. The end.

Only it isn't that simple.

While many scholars agree that Persia, Greece, pagan Rome, and Christian Rome all play parts in this vision as it makes its way to the end of time, they *don't* agree on which parts of the vision refer to which of these powers. Not only does Daniel 11:4–45 contain prophesies of some of the great conflicts of world history, but it precipitates some great fights among theologians and historians.

Because the time span that Daniel 11 covers is so great and the prophecy is so detailed, people can drown themselves in names and dates. It's like my parents trying to sort out who started it among us siblings—the answer is not always as simple as it seems that it should be. To give you the big picture, I've summarized the major interpretations of verses 4 through 45 of Daniel 11. (You can find more detailed accounts in the books I recommend at the back of this book.)

Three routes through Daniel 11

When my parents planned our family vacations, they had a tried and true route that they usually took. However, there were other ways to get to our destination too. Below are three major routes people take when they're trying to get to the end of Daniel 11.

1. The traditional route. People commonly consider the "king of the north" and

Notes

the "king of the south" whose conflicts are described in Daniel 11:5–13 to be Ptolemy and Seleucus, two of the four generals who followed Alexander. Ptolemy governed Egypt, which was south of Daniel's homeland, and—you guessed it—Seleucus possessed the north, which included Babylon, Syria, and Persia. They and their descendants spent several years after the division of Alexander's empire fighting each other in a deadly game of Touched You Last. They tried to make their dynasties get along peacefully by marrying their children to each other, but that strategy collapsed, and they continued fighting.

The traditional interpretation sees Rome breaking onto the scene in verses 14–20. This empire, a power no one can defeat, establishes itself in the "glorious land" (Daniel's homeland). Then, in verses 21 through 39, the traditional view sees Rome becoming "Christian" and taking on the characteristics of the little horn. This power is described as a "contemptible person" who uses "flattery" and attacks the "prince of the covenant"—an allusion to Christ and His ministry in the sanctuary in heaven. Scholars who follow the traditional route consider verses 25–30 to be referring to the Crusades—wars instigated by the Catholic Church, which thought the loving thing to do was to attack Muslims in an effort aimed at reclaiming various important places they felt the Muslims had taken away from Christians.

I mean, nothing says good Christian love better than lopping off someone's head, right?

Next, Daniel sees this same power "[exalting] himself and [magnifying] himself above every god" and speaking "astonishing things against the God of gods" (verse 36), which parallels the little horn of Daniel 7 and 8 and its efforts to set itself up as divine.

This section of Daniel 11 has portrayed what the traditional approach believes to be the medieval Roman Church and its sacrilegious shenanigans. Now the vision of Daniel 11 propels us, in verses 40 through 45, to the "time of the end." In this passage, we are once again greeted by the "king of the north" and the "king of the south," only now these terms refer to the powers that will be squabbling among themselves just before Jesus comes.

So, the traditional view sees the north, in verses 40–45, as symbolizing a form of Christianity that used its political and military firepower to "convert" people to its form of religion. (Remember, in Daniel's time, Babylon was north of the homeland of the people who claimed to be worshipers of God.) And the traditional view sees the king of the south as representing spiritual Egypt (verse 43), which symbolized man-made power. (In the Exodus story, Pharaoh refused to acknowledge any god but himself.) Therefore, people who accept this interpretation see the south as symbolizing secular and atheistic powers that put their trust in human reason alone. In the end, the north defeats the south and sets up camp. In other words, it takes control of the earth for the time being.

In summary, the traditional approach says the following:

- The Persian Empire will last through four more kings, and then Greece will take over (Daniel 11:1–3).
- Alexander the Great, the Greek conqueror of Persia, will expire almost immediately; leaving his empire to four of his generals (verses 4).
- General Ptolemy (and his offspring) to the north and General Seleucus (and his offspring) to the south will slap each other around for a while (verses 5–13).
- Rome will take over and do some damage (verses 14–20).
- Rome will become Christian, after a fashion, and Christian Rome will become political, obscuring Jesus' role as Savior and fighting "holy wars" with Muslims as well as with other Christians who don't subscribe to Rome's doctrines (verses 21–39).
- In the end, a political Christianity will seek to convert or kill people everywhere, and it will come into conflict with another undesirable force that holds to human reason alone (verses 40–45).

Study Questions

What do you think of the idea that the end-time king of the south represents Islam? If that interpretation is correct, how should we relate to people who are believers in Islam? What impact should their being "people of the book" (a phrase that refers to the biblical connection of Jews, Christians, and Muslims) have on what we think of them and how we treat them?

2. The traditional route—with a slight detour. Another route follows, for the most part, the traditional route, but makes a small change. It doesn't see the kings of the north and south as being Ptolemy's peeps and Seleucus's society. Instead, it sees Rome coming into the prophecy right away, in verse 4, which says that Alexander's kingdom is handed over to "other besides these." This approach says this phrase points to Rome rather than to the four Greek generals. The terms *north* and *south,* then, become symbols for all earthly space, which fits with Rome's extensive conquests. Though this route differs in this respect from the traditional route, it holds to the same picture of the end time, with the powers of the north and the south representing, on one hand, a political-religious system, and on the other, a secular human power.

3. An alternate route. Recently, a third way has been proposed that is generating much discussion among those traveling the theological highways of Daniel 11. Those who take this route propose that the end-time king of the south doesn't represent secular human power. Instead, it represents Islam.

The supporters of this route ask, "What do all the areas that make up the kingdom of the south [Egypt and other countries in the area] have in common as we near the prophesied end of time?" In other words, since Rome has come and gone, we are living near the time represented in the last parts of the visions of Daniel 2 and 7—and likely 11. So, what do the countries in this area—the Middle East—have in common now? The answer is that they all profess the Islamic faith.

Christians have much in common with Islam, its founder being a descendant of Abraham (through Ishmael; see Genesis 16). But Christians and Muslims differ regarding Jesus Christ. Muslims (the followers of Islam) believe Jesus was a great prophet—and nothing more. But Christians believe Jesus to be God, which Muslims consider blasphemous. Naturally, this has led to explosive confrontations—and that fits Daniel 11 very well.

CHAPTER 17 IN BRIEF

Just before Jesus ascended to heaven, His disciples asked Him when He would return to set up His kingdom. He replied, "It is not for you to know times or seasons which the Father has fixed by his own authority" (Acts 1:7). That's a frustrating answer—and a humbling one. There are some things we just won't know. Even Daniel, the person to whom God gave the vision, didn't live long enough to see how everything would be fulfilled.

Dr. Mervyn Maxwell, an authority on the subject of prophecy, noted, "For some Christians, matching history to this particular prophecy [Daniel 11] has become a religious diversion, even a lifelong passion, more fascinating and far more rewarding than doing jigsaw . . . or crossword puzzles."[1] Continuing this thought a few pages later, he warned, "As to the precise events on earth that will accompany their fulfillment [referring to matters prophesied in Daniel 11], wisdom suggests that we may not know them until they actually take place."[2]

These warnings tell us why the big picture on the box is so important when we're trying to figure out how puzzle pieces fit together. We may not get each piece in exactly the right place, but we can know the big idea—which is that no matter how confusing the conflicts become, God is in control of history.

There have been battles between good and evil, Christ and Satan, ever since Adam and Eve sinned, and the conflict will continue till the end of time. When you're caught in the middle (like Daniel's homeland), the world can be terrifying. But God knows about the frightening times, the confusing times, the times when the world seems to be at the mercy of violent people. Gabriel, Daniel's angel interpreter, affirmed all the prophecies Daniel had heard from the day he interpreted Nebuchadnezzar's dream and on. He assured Daniel that life on earth still moved according to God's will.

All of us face battles. We find ourselves stuck between squabbling friends, family members, classmates, and coworkers. Conflict is unavoidable, so we need to remember that conflict isn't a sign that God has abandoned us. Instead, it's a reminder for us to trust that God knows what He is doing even in the midst of the conflict. He revealed that truth to Daniel, and He reveals that truth to us as we learn from Daniel's experiences and from the prophecies God has given us through him.

ENDNOTES

1. C. Mervyn Maxwell, *The Message of Daniel,* vol. 1 of *God Cares* (Mountain View, Calif.: Pacific Press®, 1981).
2. Ibid., 297.

Chapter 18
Knockout
(Daniel 12)

Randy Couture planned to end his career with a bang on April 30, 2011.

Randy was a Greco-Roman wrestling specialist and a legend in the world of mixed martial arts. Intense training had prepared him to dish out devastating attacks and to survive brutal assaults. But Randy was forty-seven years old, so he decided this fight would be his last. He expected to win. But so did his opponent.

Lyoto Machida, a young karate and Brazilian jujitsu specialist, needed to beat Randy. When he first began to fight, Lyoto was labeled undefeatable. In his first sixteen fights, he had a record of sixteen wins and zero losses. However, he had lost his last two fights, and that had stripped him not only of his championship belt, but also of his confidence.

This match, then, was important to both fighters. Randy wanted to go out on top, and Lyoto needed a win to get back on track. As the clash of these two famous fighters drew near, the anticipation of the fans grew. This match promised to be an exciting one.

There are several ways to win a bout. One is simply for one fighter to land more blows than the other does. When the match ends, the judges tote up the damage each fighter has done, deliberate for a few minutes, and then declare one the winner. People cheer. Money is awarded. And that's that.

More impressively, a fighter can win by locking his opponent in a choke hold or any one of countless other holds and applying pressure till the opponent signals the referee to end the fight. Naturally, it's harder to get a win this way since all these fighters are as tough as nails, and no one wants to give up. But sometimes the pain becomes too intense for even these professionals to bear.

The most impressive way a fighter can win a match is with a KO—a "knockout." To get one, he has to land a blow so powerful and so perfectly placed that it literally knocks the opponent out cold, dropping him to the mat like a sack of soggy oatmeal.

Study Question

Daniel never understood everything contained in the prophecies he recorded; he had to content himself with trusting God. In what way might we face the same challenge today?

_____

_____

_____

_____

_____

_____

_____

_____

_____

_____

_____

_____

_____

_____

_____

_____

_____

_____

_____

_____

_____

(The apostle Paul compared himself to a boxer who makes every punch count; see 1 Corinthians 9:26.)

Randy and Lyoto fought an intense first round, whaling on each other with fists and feet until both were bruised and bleeding. The second round began where the first left off, but just over a minute into that round a powerful move ended the fight. Lyoto leapt into the air and launched a lightning-fast kick at Randy. His foot struck Randy in the face, knocking out several of his teeth.

Randy's eyes crossed.

He fell backwards.

Lights out.

Another decisive blow

Daniel 11 ends with the world facing its final round. Wars have been raging for centuries, and it looks as though the forces of evil are about to be declared the winner. The events portrayed in verses 40–45 of this chapter are said to occur at the "time of the end." The king of the south attacks the king of the north, but the north's army drives him south again—back into his homeland. The victory of the king of the north makes it appear that he is about to take control of the whole earth. But in the very last verse of chapter 11, Gabriel says otherwise: "He [the king of the north] shall pitch his palatial tents between the sea and the glorious holy mountain; yet he shall come to his end, with none to help him" (verse 45). That's a promise of a decisive knockout.

In Daniel 12, Gabriel continues to picture the future, finishing the vision introduced in Daniel 10 and continued through Daniel 11. He says, "At that time shall arise Michael, the great prince who has charge of your people. And there shall be a time of trouble, such as never has been since there was a nation till that time; but at that time your people shall be delivered, every one whose name shall be found written in the book" (Daniel 12:1).

The Hebrew word translated "arise" is *amad*. This word is scattered throughout chapter 11, when all of earth's powers "rise" to fight each other (see Daniel 11:6–8, 11, 13–17, 20, 21, 25, 31). But it's Michael who "*amads*" last. The throws, holds, and blows used in mixed martial arts have charming names like Guillotine, Cobra, and Eye Gouge. But in the cosmic battle between God and Satan, between Michael and the powers of the world influenced by the devil, the winning blow is the *amad*.

When Michael stands up—when He arises—it is as both military Commander and Judge. The text indicates that Michael stands up the way a victor stands over a defeated opponent.

Michael has given the knockout blow.

He's ended the fight.

Time of trouble

The Guinness Book of World Records lists what is believed to be the longest fight in history. It was a bare-knuckle battle that took place in Australia in 1855. While the average fight is measured in minutes (and sometimes only seconds), this one went on for six and a quarter hours. Surprisingly, or perhaps not so surprisingly, no one knows the name of the winner. I can only imagine the state the two fighters were in when their battle finally ended—raw, bloody, bruised, and barely alive.

No doubt those men considered their battle to be an exhausting "time of trouble" —intense in every way. The final chapter of Daniel says that when Michael stands up, there will be a "time of trouble" (a big fight) unlike any the world has ever seen. The battle between good and evil being fought on planet Earth will surge into its final round.

The angel interpreter tells Daniel that his people won't be mere spectators who watch the physical and spiritual brawls of this life from ringside seats. No, they'll be in the ring themselves. But Gabriel also tells Daniel that his people will be delivered before the battle takes their lives. Not only does God show up at the end to finish the fight for His people, but when it's over, "many of those who sleep in the dust of the earth shall awake" (verse 2).

Those who have fallen while fighting for God's cause are given eternal life. They're like decorated warriors being ushered into a Hall of Fame. The ones who picked quarrels with God's people awake to eternal shame—like tae kwon do competitor Angel Matos, who kicked a referee in the head during the 2008 Beijing Olympics and then was himself kicked out of ever competing again.

Stars and smarts

When I was a little kid, my Sabbath School teachers did everything they could to encourage me to memorize Bible verses. One of their incentives consisted of a large chart and colored stars. The color of the star we received each week indicated how well we recited our memory verse. Red meant we didn't know what we were talking about, but our hearts were in the right place. Blue meant we got a few of the words right—such as "the," "a," and "is." Silver meant we knew the verse well but didn't know the reference. And gold meant we had it all down pat.

Sabbath School scholars who collected a specified number of stars received prizes—usually candy. I regularly scored a silver or a gold star, but my teacher shouldn't have given me candy. More than once my brothers and I were sent to our parents because our hyperactivity was disrupting the class. Once when I was in kindergarten I said my memory verse flawlessly—while "sitting" upside down in my chair. My teachers were thrilled.

The next verse says, "Those who are wise shall shine like the brightness of the firmament; and those who turn many to righteousness, like the stars for ever and ever" (verse 3). In other words, God awards star status to those who know stuff.

What stuff are they supposed to know?

The next verse gives us a clue: "But you, Daniel, shut up the words, and seal the

Study Question

What purpose do times of trouble serve in the lives of God's people? (Read James 1:1–4.)

Study Question

Throughout his life Daniel was a "star" shining a light on what God was doing in the world. How can you and I shine our lights (see Matthew 5:14) on God's work in the world today?

book, until the time of the end. Many shall run to and fro, and knowledge shall increase" (verse 4). So, Daniel is told to seal up everything he's been shown because it's meant for the distant future. Then the verse says there will be an explosion of information in that distant future, which is near the time of the end. A lot of people think Gabriel was pointing to the rapid increase in technological wonders in the past century or so. They look at everything we can do and deduce that this means we're living in the time of the end.

That's an interesting observation. We certainly have cool gadgets aplenty. With my iPhone not only can I communicate with people around the world, but I can also search the Internet and access just about any piece of information I could ever need—or want (such as the reference for my memory verse). We have a knowledge overload. There's a digital world within our physical one that lets people explore virtually (pun intended) everything. Some people's friendships are built entirely on online chats or constant tweet and status updates.

However, this verse isn't speaking primarily of general information. Skipping ahead to verse 10, we read, "Many shall purify themselves, and make themselves white, and be refined; but the wicked shall do wickedly; and none of the wicked shall understand; but those who are wise shall understand." Wisdom involves understanding—and not just random useless facts (such as how a snail can sleep for three years—thanks Google).

In this passage, what those who are wise understand is Daniel's prophecies. They are wise because they know God's counsel and trust His plans rather than the schemes of power-hungry human rulers. The big idea is that the increase of knowledge and understanding that God considers significant is the knowledge about and understanding of Daniel's prophecies. Those who understand those prophecies will be God's stars.

Cliffhanger

Daniel is certainly one of God's stars. But when it comes to understanding the entire vision of chapters 10 through 12, well, God doesn't explain it all to him. Daniel is told to "shut up the words" of the prophecy because they aren't for his time (verse 4). This probably didn't make Daniel feel real shiny and starlike.

Then Daniel sees Michael (clothed in linen) and hears someone ask Him how long it will be to the "end of these wonders" (verses 5, 6). Michael takes a solemn oath, raising both His hands toward heaven, and He points the questioner to the "time, two times, and half a time" (verse 7), which brings to mind the timeline discussed in Daniel 7. However, when it comes to any more details regarding the time of the end, Daniel says, "I heard, but I did not understand" (verse 8).

Daniel asks for more information regarding the prophecy, but he's told, "Go your way, . . . for the words are shut up and sealed until the time of the end" (verse 9).

Sorry, Daniel—the book is shut for another time.

As I write this, the final book of a series I have been reading has been released. Everyone who has been reading this series has been waiting for this book. It has taken the author years to complete—leaving all his readers pulling their hair out because the third book ended in a cliffhanger. (*Cliffhanger* is a literary term for a book or story that ends with someone in a precarious position and doesn't tell how things turn out. *Frazzled* is a psychological term describing readers who have just read a cliffhanger.)

Hanging from a physical cliff is, to me, unpleasant. Being caught up in a good story and then having to wait to find out what happens is worse. At least when you're hanging from a cliff, the agony can't go on for years.

Daniel's story ends in a cliffhanger too. Even Daniel himself wouldn't understand everything until he is resurrected when Michael arises at the end of time.

The 1,290 and 1,335 days

There's no consensus among scholars as to what the prophetic timelines given in Daniel 12:11, 12 mean. Verse 11 speaks of "continual burnt offerings" and the "abomination that makes desolate." This language ties these timelines to the events that Daniel 8 portrays. (Remember our friend *tamid*?)

Daniel 8 features the longest prophetic timeline—the 2,300 days, which ended in 1844. There are scholars who use that date to make sense of the 1,290 days/years (Daniel 12:11) and the 1,335 days/years (Daniel 12:12). Subtracting 1,335 from 1843, the year Miller first set as the time of Christ's return, gives us the date of 508—which was the year the little horn defeated the three barbarian tribes (see Daniel 7). And adding 1,290 to 508 brings us to 1798, when the pope was taken captive and died in prison, which significantly lessened the power of the little horn for a while.

The truth is that while this calculation ties in nicely with the dates we have discussed in previous chapters, not everyone agrees that's what these time periods are about. This simply means there is more for you and me to study as knowledge about the prophecies of Daniel continues to increase.

CHAPTER 18 IN BRIEF

Daniel 12 is the shortest chapter in the book. It concludes the vision begun in chapter 10. Michael (Jesus) takes a stand at the end of the world's conflicts and delivers the final blow on behalf of His people. God's people go through a time of trouble, but they are delivered and given eternal life, while those who have fought against God's purposes are eternally shamed. Then Daniel is told to seal the vision.

While Daniel desperately wants to know all the details, he is told only the outcome: God will save His people. Daniel has to go to his grave trusting that all will end well when this world's conflicts are finished.

Study Question

There's more for us to find in Daniel's prophecies. What would be a good next step toward exploring subjects like the 1,335 days and the 1,290 days?

_____

_____

_____

_____

_____

_____

_____

_____

_____

_____

_____

_____

_____

_____

_____

_____

_____

_____

_____

_____

_____

_____

God didn't intend Bible prophecy to reveal every minute detail of what will happen in the future. He meant it primarily to assure believers that He will not only stand by His people through all times of trouble, but that He will ultimately bring all fighting to an end and grant eternal life to His followers. God has given us enough detail to strengthen our faith when we are struggling to make sense of the world and to believe God is in control, but ultimately, we still need to have faith in God and not feel that we will know every fact and facet of the final fight. By all accounts we are living at the time of the end. Conflicts of every conceivable kind abound. Prophecy has never been more relevant, and we need to take it more seriously and to put more time and effort into studying it. There is more for you to discover and share with those around you. Take the time to dig further into the details this prophetic book contains. Who knows what you will find?

Chapter 19
Judge Jesus

Television does a good job of portraying judges as some of the most frightening people on the globe.

Judges have the power to decree people as innocent or guilty and to apply penalties, so they're plenty petrifying enough; but when you also give them a license to sass, they become even more alarming. Judge Judy and Judge Joe Brown, two of the most well-known "reality television" judges, use that license freely. For instance, when someone in the court offered an opinion, Judge Judy furrowed her brow and barked, "I don't care what you think! I'm the one who has to determine what is fair!"

Yikes.

And on another occasion, Judge Judy narrowed her cold eyes and yelled, "If you live to be a hundred, you will never be as smart as me. On your *best* day, you're not as smart as I am on my *worst* day."

Ouch!

It's never a good idea to interrupt a judge. Should you try, you might hear something akin to what Judge Judy told one motormouth while holding her gavel in a white-knuckled grip: "Two people can't talk at the same time. When my mouth is moving, it means that you need to be quiet."

One of my favorite interactions occurred when Judge Judy asked a defendant what they did for a living. Their response: "Um."

Without missing a beat, Judge Judy bared her teeth and attacked, " 'Um' is not an answer! What kind of training did you need to do 'Um'?"

Judge Judy doesn't take any nonsense—nor do other judges. On one occasion, the deep voice of Judge Joe Brown—another television personality—let one woman know the effect she was having on him. "You are an irritant, lady," he said. "You're irritating me!"

And when one young man protested what Judge Brown was saying, the judge roared, "Son, close your mouth. I'm trying to give you some necessary man-training, so one day you can become a man."

Human judges wield a lot of power and can be extremely intimidating. Matter of fact, there's an old saying we use when people get in trouble. We tell them they're "going to face the judge." A judge on planet Earth can assign a plethora of punishments, ranging from warnings and fines to execution.

For this reason, the thought of Jesus—God—as a judge is terrifying because He holds the power to sentence people to *eternal* life or death.

However, Daniel offers us hope.

We've already explored Daniel 7—but I've saved a piece of it for this last chapter because I feel it's the most encouraging picture in the entire book. In Daniel 7, Jesus appears as a judge just after the little horn begins speaking great things. The scene is nothing short of awesome. A circle of thrones surrounds the seat of the Ancient of Days. His hair is white, and so are His clothes—and His seat (throne) is completely enflamed (Daniel 7:9). "A stream of fire issued and came out from before him; a thousand thousands served him, and ten thousand times ten thousand stood before him; the court sat in judgment, and the books were opened" (verse 10).

A court far more intimidating than Judge Judy's was opening its session. Some serious judging was about to take place.

The text goes on to say that "one like a son of man" comes in the clouds and is "given dominion and glory and kingdom," and that everyone will serve Him (verses 13, 14). The New Testament records show that "Son of man" is a title Jesus often applied to Himself. Jesus is the One who is given authority to judge.

The books are open

In the story *Willy Wonka and the Chocolate Factory,* children are promised a magical trip to a mythical candy factory—if they can find a golden ticket. Wonka, the slightly insane chocolatier, hides the tickets in a handful of candy bars. Throughout the narrative, vast multitudes tear open countless bars of chocolate in hopes of finding a ticket. But most of the kids find only chocolate. Just a select few are lucky enough to find that sweet golden ticket.

Too many Christians fear that they're about as likely to find their name in God's book as they are to find one of Wonka's golden tickets. They see God as a cruel judge bent on destroying everyone He can. They think God eliminates all those who disobey Him, and all of us, if we're honest, can think of moments in life when we blew it.

So, even for numerous believers who place their faith in God despite their shortcomings, judgment is a scary concept. But Daniel's vision clarifies what judgment is all about.

The little horn makes war against the saints "until the Ancient of Days came, and judgment was given *for the saints* of the Most High, and the time came when the saints received the kingdom" (verse 22; emphasis added).

Did you catch that? Judgment is *for* the saints.

It's in *their favor.*
Judge Jesus defends His people and rules against the forces of evil.
Judge Jesus saves His people.
We don't have to fear God's judgment.

CHAPTER 19 IN BRIEF

The devil aims to fill our hearts with doubt so we will abandon hope in the future God is leading us into. He aims to distract us with the pain and suffering we see around us. That can make us feel despair and cause us to wonder if we should abandon belief in a divine plan. But prophecy—especially the prophecies in Daniel and Revelation—tells us to stay on God's side through whatever conflicts may come.

At its core, the book of Daniel is about the great battle between God and evil. While Daniel sees the evil his people will suffer, he also sees that God will eventually intervene and put an end to all pain and suffering.

And Daniel sets us a good example. While he is frustrated both at what his people will have to endure and at his lack of understanding of God's plan, he never once doubts that God will take care of them. And God does. He shows up in the heat of the battle and executes judgment for His people.

Daniel's prophecies tell us that we have no reason to fear the future when our faith is in Jesus.

Recommended Reading

Doukhan, Jacques. *Secrets of Daniel: Wisdom and Dreams of a Jewish Prince in Exile.* Hagerstown, Md.: Review and Herald® Publishing Association, 2000. Written by one of my seminary professors, this great book gives a unique, Jewish perspective on the book of Daniel and presents some interesting insights from the Hebrew and Aramaic in which Daniel was written.

Finley, Mark. *The Next Superpower.* Hagerstown, Md.: Review and Herald®, 2005. This easy-to-read book gives a good general overview of biblical prophecy.

Maxwell, C. Mervyn. *God Cares,* vol. 1. Mountain View, Calif.: Pacific Press® Publishing Association, 1981. This very detailed book is a standard work in Seventh-day Adventist interpretation of Daniel. I recommend it highly.

Roosenberg, Tim. *Islam and Christianity in Prophecy.* Hagerstown, Md.: Review and Herald®, 2011. The most recently published book in my list, this one explores the role of Islam in Bible prophecy, particularly in Daniel 11.

Shea, William. *The Abundant Life Bible Amplifier: Daniel 7–12.* Nampa, Idaho: Pacific Press®, 1996. Use this book as a study guide as you read the difficult final chapters of Daniel.

Smith, Uriah. *Daniel and the Revelation.* Hagerstown, Md.: Review and Herald®, 2005. Written more than one hundred years ago, this is the original benchmark book on prophecy for the Seventh-day Adventist Church. While the church's scholars on Daniel and Revelation now disagree with some of the interpretations posed by this book, it still remains a classic, and most still agree with its general approach.

Stefanovic, Zdravko. *Daniel: Wisdom to the Wise.* Nampa, Idaho: Pacific Press®, 2007. Ranko Stefanovic wrote the most recent Seventh-day Adventist verse-by-verse commentary on the book of Revelation. Zdravko, his brother, followed with this commentary on Daniel. It is a balanced offering that goes through each chapter in detail and then makes everyday, practical applications. It's a nice addition to your budding library on prophecy.